MY ANCE: WERE JEWISH

HOW CAN I FIND OUT MORE ABOUT THEM?

by Dr Anthony Joseph, MA (Cantab), FSG

SOCIETY OF GENEALOGISTS ENTERPRISES LTD

Published by
Society of Genealogists Enterprises Limited
14 Charterhouse Buildings
Goswell Road
London EC1M 7BA

First Edition 1982 as My Ancestor was Jewish, by Isobel Mordy
Second Edition 1995 © The Society of Genealogists
Third Edition © Dr Anthony Joseph 2002

ISBN 1 903462 63 0

British Library Cataloguing in Publication Data
A CIP Catalogue record for this book is available from the British Library

About the Author
Formerly a West Midlands General Practitioner; past President of the Jewish
Historical Society of England; currently President of the Jewish Genealogical
Society of Great Britain; corresponding member for Great Britain of the
Australian Jewish Historical Society; sometime member of the Board of the
International Association of Jewish Genealogical Societies and Life Member
of the Society of Genealogists since 1955.

Society of Genealogists Enterprises Limited is a wholly owned subsidiary of
Society of Genealogists, a registered charity, no 233701

Cover illustration - Ketubah (marriage contract) of Abraham Gleiberman and
Esther Weinstein, 18 March 1909, Birmingham Hebrew Congregation.
Reproduced from the author's family papers.

CONTENTS

FOREWORD

The 'My Ancestors Were ....' series has proved to be amongst the most popular set of guide books published by the Society of Genealogists.

Isobel Mordy, the author of the first edition of this booklet (originally published in 1982) died in 1993 and my obituary of her was published in the *Genealogists' Magazine* Volume 24 (September 1993), page 299. Notwithstanding her increasing infirmity during the last few months of her life, combined with failing eyesight and deteriorating mobility, she laboured on a revision of this booklet and agreed that Charles Tucker should complete it and expand and update the bibliographies.

Mr Michael Gandy, FSG, edited the earlier editions and contributed considerably to some of the chapters. As the present editor of the *Genealogists' Magazine*, and in conjunction with the Society of Genealogists generally, he has now commissioned a further update of the work and it has been my privilege to have attempted to follow in Isobel's footsteps by undertaking the task of a new revision of her original concept.

Those who have used the earlier editions will find numerous changes in this updated version. However, I have endeavoured in many respects to follow the format devised by Isobel Mordy, which I think has stood the test of time and forms a permanent memorial to her pursuit of genealogical excellence.

I would like to thank, in particular, many of the staff of the Society of Genealogists without whose encouragement and practical assistance my task would have been rendered immensely more difficult. My especial thanks to Else Churchill for her comments, suggestions and helpful advice. I am also very grateful to John Titford of the Publications Committee of the Society of Genealogists for his mentoring of my efforts.

I am more indebted than I can express to 'Avotaynu' for their generous permission for me to publish abstracts from material already offered to them as part of their *Guide to Jewish Genealogy*, which is in press. My gratitude is equally offered to Rosemary Wenzerul and Saul Issroff for their permission to use an important listing of contact addresses and websites compiled for the Jewish Genealogical Society of Great Britain's publication *Jewish Ancestors? A Beginner's Guide to Jewish Genealogy in Great Britain*.

Lastly, but by no means least, without the everyday help of my friend, genealogical secretary and audio-typist, Sheila Rawlins, this monograph could not have been produced. My very sincere thanks to her for all her work.

If this work proves to be as useful as the former editions, the credit is largely due to the very sound foundation by Isobel Mordy and the back-up from my colleagues. However, I alone am responsible for any omissions or failings.

Anthony Joseph
Birmingham
July 2002

CHAPTER 1: INTRODUCTION

In Jewish tradition, genealogy is rooted in the very origins of the people itself. In the first Book of the Bible (Genesis) much commentary is devoted to the lineage of the Patriarchs. The very definition of who is a Jew, while not capable of being narrowed down to a single concept, in the case of those born into the faith requires matrilineal proof of identity. A wise insistence on acknowledgement of the mother for basic Judaic inheritance dates from the earliest times and this has skilfully blended with paternal transmission in such matters as the handing on of land and the priesthood. Early Jewish thinking demonstrates a lucid grasp of the nature of some genetic disorders; for example the laws pertaining to ritual circumcision were modified in cases of haemorrhagic illnesses in such a way that all potentially-affected males of that family would be spared exposure to the risk of bleeding. Had Queen Victoria's advisors possessed such an adequate comprehension of these matters, the course of modern Russian history might have been profoundly altered. [1]

Scholars from many disciplines have written about Jewish people, their migrations (by no means always voluntarily) in and out of many countries, and about their beliefs, customs and traditions. It is important to understand this background before attempting to trace Jewish ancestry. Inevitably with so many movements from country to country, following the elusive threads of a family story may prove more difficult than for those whose ancestors have remained within the confines of a settled geographical and/or historical unit. Bearing this in mind, the Anglo-Jewish community has been an important part of the fabric of worldwide Jewry and has had a significant presence in its own right. Moreover, it has also proved one of the pivotal staging posts for a very large number of migrant Jews leaving Russia (and many other parts of Eastern Europe) on their journeys towards their perception of a better destination: the United States of America. Although the USA received the largest percentage of these migrants, significant numbers also came through the UK and ended up in countries such as Canada, South Africa, Australia and New Zealand. It may be noted in passing that the development of steam-powered vessels in the 19th century made it possible to move large numbers of people across oceans cheaply and in relative comfort. As a result, the mass migration of Europeans in the 19th and early part of the 20th centuries progressed on a vast scale. Between 1830 and 1914, perhaps 60 million passengers made the voyage from Europe to the USA and this included something like five million Jews. Many of these people left a Northern European port and settled directly on the Eastern Seaboard of Canada and the USA, but many more also found themselves in the UK with the possibility of their having left at least some record of their passage through Britain. It is, therefore, frequently useful to examine English records in the hope of discovering details about European migrants even if their presence in the UK was only temporary.

Precisely when the first Jews arrived in Britain is unknown. It has been speculated there may have been Jews here in Roman times and even before that. However, the first proven date of settlement is 1066: the time of the well-known arrival of William I of Normandy (known as William the Conqueror). William brought with him an entourage from the Normandy French Jewish Community which had been well-established for some time as financiers to his Court. Their banking and kindred skills were of as much use to William in England as they had been in Normandy, France. The Medieval Anglo-Jewish Community persisted in varying fortunes for rather more than two centuries and for the most part was tolerated as an acceptable ethnic minority. From time to time popular feeling erupted against the Jews, leading to such terrible massacres as that at York in 1189. On occasion, if deaths occurred somewhere in the English countryside under apparently suspicious circumstances, especially if a child was involved, grotesque blood libels were promulgated and the Jews became scapegoats. This process became more intense in the latter part of the 13th century where increasing hostility to the perceived powers of the Jewish financiers led to the Edict of Expulsion by an Act of Edward I. This was implemented on 1st August 1290 and the entire Anglo-Jewish population at that time either fled the country, became forcibly baptised or were put to death.

Between 1290 and 1656 (a period of rather more than three-and-a-half centuries) very few Jews resided in or visited England. An occasional traveller such as Sir Edward Brampton (in reality a Portuguese Jewish adventurer called Edvardo Brandao) makes a footnote in British history, but there were certainly no Jewish religious or communal institutions and no cohesive presence such as had obtained in the Medieval period. In Elizabethan times, small numbers of Portuguese Jews immigrated to London but practised their religion only in secret. These were Sephardim and the distinction between this group of Jews and their other brethren, known as Ashkenazim, will be explained shortly. On the surface they were as Christian as their neighbours, because of concerns about the penalty for 'heresy'. This clandestine Jewish Community (sometimes known as 'Marranos' which means pigs) derived from Jews of the Iberian Peninsula, who had fled from the Edicts of Spain (1492) and Portugal (1496). They had been forcibly converted to Christianity under penalty of death. They did have some influence in Elizabethan English ruling circles. A well-known exemplar of this period was the physician to Queen Elizabeth I, Ruy Lopez, who was also a chess expert. During the first half of the 17th century, the numbers of Marranos slowly increased; although many of Portuguese background arrived via Holland, with the advancing of Anglo-Dutch trading between London and Amsterdam. In 1656 the Lord Protector, Oliver Cromwell, received a Petition from a Portuguese-Dutch Jew, Menasseh ben Israel, who requested the lifting of the Edict of 1290 and religious freedom for his (Jewish) people. For various reasons, partly hard-headed and practical and partly superstitious, Cromwell granted permission for the establishment of a Sephardi synagogue. This grouping, the first Community of Re-settlement, is still in existence today and is based at the Bevis Marks Synagogue in the City of London. From 1656, the covert Marrano Community was able to identify openly with the newcomers who were, for the most part, wealthy merchants. In fact, the Edict of 1290 of Edward I has never been formally repealed, but Cromwell indicated that the authorities would no longer refer to it as a tool to harass or oppress Jewish settlers.

The differences between Sephardim and Ashkenazim are rooted in matters of Jewish tradition rather than theology. The former group has evolved its customs through Spanish, Portuguese, North African and Italian backgrounds whereas the latter, major section of the Jewish people has been influenced by Eastern Europe: Russia, Poland, Lithuania and, to some extent, from German admixture. Considerable overlap between the two groups has always existed and the separate traditions have frequently flourished side-by-side in many countries such as Holland, England and France.

The successful revival of Sephardi Jewish life in Britain was rapidly followed by the arrival of the Ashkenazi Jewish settlers – mostly from Germany but a few from countries further to the east thereof. By 1690 their numbers were sufficient for them to open their first synagogue (known as the Great Synagogue) which existed in Dukes Place, London, until it was bombed in the Second World War.

It is appropriate at this point to demolish an endearing (and enduring) myth concerning the relationship between these Re-settlement 17th century Jewish congregations and the former Medieval Anglo-Jewish Community. There is absolutely no connection whatsoever between them and it is not possible to trace any modern living descendants from the Jews who lived in Britain before 1290. It is sometimes possible to trace the ancestry of Jewish families as far back as the thirteenth century (or even earlier) but they are not connected in any way with the Anglo-Jewish Medieval Community, nor do any British sources contribute to this type of research.

Between 1700 and 1900, substantial numbers of Jews immigrated to England, mostly via Holland and Germany, and then, towards the end of the 19th century, more predominantly from Eastern Europe. It has been estimated that there may have been 3,000 Jews living in England (virtually all of them in or near London) in 1700 and this had multiplied some tenfold to 30,000 by 1800. Only part of this expansion was due to natural increase, indicating that immigration led to substantial numbers of Jewish people settling here. Although London, as the Capital, proved the greatest magnet attracting would-be settlers to these shores, specific problems arose with the Guild System which controlled employment and insisted on Saturday (Sabbath) working. Guilds were much less powerful outside London, which allowed for an exodus from the Capital for religious Jews who found many difficulties placed in their way in London.

Such people moved to the small ports and country towns along the South Coast of England from Ipswich in the East to Penzance in the West. They became successful hawkers and peddlers and established small but thriving Jewish Communities in many an apparently-remote area. A base was established to which the Community members repaired for regular Sabbath observance each week. One of their number would arrive early to prepare the religious and social requirements for the others and after the Sabbath was concluded, Saturday evening, the hawking and peddling would start again by roaming the countryside to sell wares. In many cases, notably in the ports of the South Coast of England, once the Communities had become sufficiently established, direct trade occurred between many Continental towns and the Jews settled in the various parts of Southern England. This also led to further immigration directly to these areas and the Jewish peddler, often on horseback, became a familiar sight in the 18th century English countryside. After the Industrial Revolution and with many changes in the economic working habits of society, the hawking and peddling communities began to decline rapidly. However, traces of the colourful Jewish contribution to local life can sometimes still be found. An occasional building, defunct Jewish cemetery or memorial are yet identifiable.

In the first half of the 19th century, continued natural increase and immigration gave rise to the establishment of the large Provincial Communities in cities such as Manchester, Liverpool, Leeds, Bristol and Birmingham. The latter half of the 19th century formed the period of major mass immigration, fuelled partly by economic misery in the countries of origin and partly by religious oppression in Russia, Russian Poland and Romania. This flood of migration to England at that time gave rise to many concerns as to how many such people could be 'absorbed', and the restrictive effect of the Aliens' Act 1905 curbed but did not abolish the number of Jews attempting to arrive here. The 'threat' of such mass arrival of desperately poor people caused as much concern amongst the well-established, previously-settled Jews as within the minds of the secular authorities. Much of this intense poverty descended on the East End of London and led to the establishment by wealthy co-religionists of some charitable institutions to relieve the suffering of the new arrivals. It should be noted that the wealthy were not always as forthcoming as might have been expected. Frequently worried that the new arrivals would engender an anti-immigrant backlash that might also destabilise the well-established and (by now) more prosperous segment of the Community, the rich and powerful Jewish communal leaders often advocated minimum charity to relieve only the most needy of their brethren. They also attached 'strings' to the relief to prevent the newcomers settling permanently and encouraged them instead to move on. In contrast, organisations such as the Poor Jews' Temporary Shelter emerged with a genuine concern for the very destitute, but were in conflict with 'official' charities. The records of the Shelter are now being computerised and may be very helpful.[2]

4

The whole pattern of the movement of peoples between nations was profoundly affected by the First World War. Bureaucratic control and state management of would-be migrants became the established norm. With the rise of the Nazi domination of Europe, many Jews attempted to leave both Germany itself and the countries that Germany came to control by one technique or another. The fortunate number who did successfully depart Germany and German-controlled territories frequently arrived in Britain although, as with so many previous migrations from different parts of Europe, some were simply passengers on their way to the USA or Canada. A significant minority of these refugees also found themselves ultimately in Australia and New Zealand.

Since the end of the Second World War, Anglo-Jewry has declined numerically from perhaps its maximum of half-a-million to the present-day numbers of between 250,000 and 300,000. Even with a maximum Jewish to Gentile ratio, the proportion of Anglo-Jews has never been more than 1% of the general population. Nevertheless, this minority Community has had a considerable influence on British life and has added a colourful dimension to the nation's story.

CHAPTER 2
THE EMANCIPATION OF THE JEWS IN ENGLAND

It has been shown in the previous chapter that, since 1656, the immigration of Jews to Great Britain and their settlement there has proceeded more or less as part of general migration patterns (that is, of Jews and non-Jews) out of various parts of Europe. It has been affected by the desire for (mostly) economic advance and occasionally by the avoidance of oppression. The immigrants have been absorbed and incorporated into English national life, have adapted to the pre-existing conditions obtaining at the time and suffered little practical disadvantage. Thus the Edict of 1290 caused no impediment to the mid-17th century Jewish merchants who came from Amsterdam and made their lives thenceforth in London. For reasons that will be given later, Jews were often able to record their primary events (and did so), such as birth or death, within the parish register system.[3] Although the Guild System, with its insistence on Saturday working, caused hardship for religious Jews, it applied virtually exclusively to London and had little adverse effect outside the Capital.

Numerous professions were closed to Jews and many schools applied restrictions until late into the 19th century. Land ownership was similarly a difficulty, although the collection of local taxes such as rates was applied to whichever person or persons were living on a property. In the 17th and 18th centuries, Jews were excluded from the Freedom of the City of London (which caused difficulty for retailing) but many Jews did join the City Livery Companies. A surprising number of Jews availed themselves of insurance facilities, and the lists of policy holders from the 18th century insurance companies, held at the Guildhall Library, can be a very fruitful genealogical source.[4]

In general terms, the State viewed the Jewish Community as autonomous and self-regulating, so its dealings with the Community tended to be via such quasi-representative organisations as the Board of Deputies (established in 1760). Jews (and Quakers) were exempted from the provisions of the Hardwicke Marriage Act of 1753 which otherwise required all marriages solemnised in England and Wales to be conducted through the authority of a clergyman. The Hardwicke exemption also allowed Jewish marriages to be solemnised anywhere in the country (and not specifically in a licensed building for the purpose), a privilege which the rest of British society has only acquired in the past few years.

Political emancipation, lack of which had very little practical bearing on the lives of most of the Jews in this country, proceeded piecemeal, starting with the 'Jew Bill' of 1752 (repealed only a few months later) and continued more or less in parallel with the emancipation of other Non-Conformist groups, such as the Roman Catholics, until the removal of all civil disabilities by 1871. Admission to the Bar was allowed from 1833, participation in local government from 1845 and entry to Parliament from 1858. The final steps were the granting of permission to matriculate from Oxford University and to take a degree at Cambridge University; both of these were allowed from 1871. It is interesting to note that the theoretical difficulties preventing Jews from entering the professions or Parliament were not a result of the rules of admission to these institutions. The stumbling block was encountered at the time of administering the Oath of Loyalty which required using the phrase 'On the true faith of a Christian'. The 'Redbrick' universities, starting with University College London, have always accepted Jews, and in the case of the latter institution, its foundation was financially assisted by some of the richer members of the Jewish Community.

The so-called 'Jew Bill' was an Act of Parliament passed in 1752 to remove any applicable Jewish civil disabilities that obtained at the time and it was a reward for Joseph Salvador who had helped the government out of intense financial embarrassment. The Bill was passed but created a 'backlash' and the government was forced to repeal it in the next Parliamentary session. The spectre of banning pork butchers, etc. was waved by some of the Bishops in the House of Lords and fear of 'koshering' all the meat trade frightened Parliament into submission! It is interesting to note that at about the same time, the Hardwicke Marriage Act was successfully passed and conferred autonomy on the Jewish Community for regulating its own marriages.

Jews were admitted to the Merchant Taylors School for a time during the 18th century and to the City of London School from its re-foundation. St Paul's School, then in Hammersmith, was the first public school to accept them, and Clifton College was the first educational establishment to have a specific Jewish section (Polack House). The relevance of all this for the genealogist is that some of the old school registers may prove useful sources, as may also directories of the modern professional bodies. Many of these registers may be listed in the Society of Genealogists' holdings including its published *Guide to School Registers* which is held in the Library. Some private Jewish schools have existed since the early 19th century. There is no specific list of such schools but they may be mentioned in the *Jewish Year Book* which is published annually by the *Jewish Chronicle*.

CHAPTER 3
WHERE TO START : GENERAL PRINCIPLES

The usual starting point in any pedigree investigation is in the present and working backwards. In this context some genealogical methodology is common to all research, whether Jewish or for any other family. All available information should be accumulated from as many living sources as possible and the technique of oral history, interviewing relatives, telephone gathering of data, consulting any existing research findings, etc., is the initial impetus. Care should be taken over noting the *sources of information*, the negative points as well as the positive findings, and with clear identification. Failure to observe these rules may lead to the need to repeat much of the work already carried out in a frustrating attempt to discover the source of a story which could confirm or refute a previously-held conjecture about a family line in the light of newly-discovered information.

The compulsory (secular) registration of births, marriages and deaths began in England and Wales in 1837, in Scotland in 1855 and in Ireland in 1864. Although never a voluntary system, many such primary events did escape registration in the early years of its operation. A principal reason for this was the wording of the 1836 Act of William IV, which set out the rules and regulations and imposed the duty of discovering events on the Superintendent Registrars for each administrative locality. Since the Registrar was paid for the entries recorded, a financial incentive existed to list the same information twice or even more. It was also possible to create totally fictitious entries, and on occasions the temptation for a Registrar to supplement his income thereby proved irresistible. Another recording problem, with particular relevance for Jewish genealogical searching, was the lack of familiarity with the new system, which posed particular problems for relatively-new arrivals here. Eastern European Jewish immigrants, already wary of dealing with officialdom from their experiences in their countries of origin, simply omitted to report primary events to the local Registrar. It has been estimated that perhaps 10-15% of births and deaths may have escaped recording as a result of these problems, and these non-registrations are over-represented amongst the newly-immigrant population. It is, therefore, relatively common, but frustrating, not to be able to find an appropriate birth or death certificate for an individual about whom the reasonable assumption may be made that their birth or death did occur in England or Wales. In such circumstances it is always sensible to carry out a wider time-period search and also to note the possibility of siblings for the person being sought. Registration of marriages, apart from a particular problem that will be discussed in the next chapter, is probably complete.

Another important consideration in Jewish genealogical research is the variability of name recording. This could be due to non-specific spelling or to problems encountered with the dialect and pronunciation of the person supplying the information to the Registrar. It may sometimes be extremely difficult to imagine the possible spelling variations that may have ended up in the listings. Substitution of 'V' for 'W' may be easily perceived and relatively simple permutations such as Mandelson (might be Mendelson or Mindelson) or Moskovitch/Muscovitch will be solved easily enough. 'Pluralising' of names (e.g. Jacob/Jacobs, Solomon/Solomons) must also be considered because these variations may be used inconsistently over several generations. Names may also be 'reversed' so that, for example, Moses Jacob may appear as Jacob Moses. These sorts of variant factors usually emerge after due consideration, but much more difficulty may be encountered with such unexpected (and not easily thought about) spelling fluidity such as Wainstain for Weinstein or Chaltiel for Shaltiel or even Sealtiel. A phonetic soundex listing, such as that used by the IGI, would be an excellent research tool for these GRO indexes if it were ever made available.

The 1836 Registration Act was considerably tightened up by the amendment to it of 1874, which empowered midwives to report on births and placed the onus of registration of these events on the parents rather than on the local Registrar. However, even after 1874 many instances of non-registration appear to have occurred and again they are over-represented amongst the immigrant Jewish Community, many of whom flooded into Britain in the last twenty years of the 19th century.

CHAPTER 4: MARRIAGES

It has been noticed in chapter 2 that Hardwicke's Marriage Act of 1753, subsequently amended by the Marriage Act of 1823, exempted Jews and Quakers from its provisions. Jewish marriages certainly could be solemnised in synagogues but also in any other place if so desired by the participants. A tradition of using a private house (frequently that of the bride) or public places such as taverns, coffee houses and the like, is still popular with the Jewish Community. An example discovered some time ago was a marriage which took place in a concert hall; the bride was a singer. After compulsory civil registration (from July 1837), marriage certificates normally stated the address at which the marriage had taken place, although sometimes the important exact details are lacking and the address is simply given as a general area. If the address does not immediately appear to be the bride's, it may be that of a near relative or friend and it is always worthwhile finding out who was living at the address at the time, either through census returns or through directories. While the name of the occupant may not be clearly that of a relative, a little investigation will sometimes reveal that there has been a change of name or another kinsperson's marriage of which one had previously been unaware.

Although the English Courts appear to have always recognised Jewish marriages as being valid in law, no interest was taken by the authorities in enforcing a system of registration prior to the introduction of the national civil registration system. Thereafter, duly certified synagogues maintained their registers and sent in their returns to the Registrar General in precisely the same manner as other denominations. The Orthodox Jewish Community itself demanded for a long time that all Jewish marriages, whether of their own members or of other Jewish groupings (such as the Reform Community), be recorded via the Orthodox Returns and sent on to the Registrar General. This gave rise to considerable ill-feeling between different segments of the Jewish Community in that the Reform and Progressive elements were dissatisfied with having their affairs supervised by the Orthodox Community. It was also possible, under this system, for the Orthodox grouping to refuse to sanction a marriage if they did not approve of the religious provenance under which it was solemnised or, more particularly, if they were not satisfied that one or both parties to the marriage were Jewish. From time to time the problem was resolved by Act of Parliament, empowering the Registrar General to authorise non-Orthodox groupings to hold a licence for solemnising marriages. It may be noted, in passing, that many of the secular counterpart marriage certificates submitted to the Registrar General were signed by one or both of the participants making a mark (usually a circle). It has been suggested that this proves considerable illiteracy amongst the immigrant Jewish population, but a more likely explanation is that the languages spoken and written by the Jewish bride and/or groom would normally have been written in Hebrew script, which was not allowed by the English civil authorities on secular documentation. It has also been noticed that frequently the bride and groom appeared to have been living at the same address at the time of a marriage. This has given rise to speculation that many such marriages had, in fact, taken place under Jewish religious law before the secular ceremony was also performed. Here, too, this is unlikely, and usually such religious and secular marriages followed each other closely. The explanation for only one address being given was that it reduced the costs of the exercise if the statutory fees for civil marriage only involved one parish.

However, the possibility of a Jewish marriage having been solemnised only in accordance with Jewish religious practice is very real and explains why, in many cases, no marriage for a couple can apparently be identified in the secular registers. Jews who used this tradition would satisfy their religious conscience and would feel perfectly comfortable living with each other as man and wife in such circumstances. However, the Registrar General did not approve of the practice since it undermined the concept of civil marriage as part of the fabric of society. No duly licensed synagogue sanctioned such marriages and if connivance at the practice was discovered, penalties were applied. Nevertheless, the practice was quite widespread, being known as 'stille chuppah' ('silent marriage') and of course, resulted in a lack of centrally-indexed documentation that can be used to track down the participants.

In Jewish religious custom, a marriage is valid if solemnised in the presence of two religiously-fit Jewish witnesses and if a marriage contract (ketubah) is then issued to the bride. Prior to the secular civil registration system, the ketubah may be the only evidence of a marriage, and if the supporting documentation copies have not been kept with the synagogue, it may be impossible to discover any further details. The practice of lodging a duplicate copy of the ketubah with the archives of the Congregation issuing it only became widespread after the middle of the latter part of the 19th century.

Chapters 5 and 6 will show the value of the *Gentleman's Magazine* for Jewish genealogical research, and many of the news items in that publication referred to marriages, especially amongst the more wealthy among the Jewish Community. Reference will also be made in chapter 9 to the death of Rosceia Lazarus that appeared in an issue of the *Lincolnshire, Stamford and Rutland Mercury* in April 1832; and a splendid (and very detailed) account of her marriage on 5th August 1810 in Godmanchester is an excellent example of the quality of the *Gentleman's Magazine's* reporting. Various newspapers, notably the London *Jewish Chronicle*, founded in 1841, have had regular announcements of births, marriages and deaths. The quality of the data recorded is, of course, variable, as with any newspaper production. Quite recently, Doreen Berger has abstracted all these relevant details (and much more useful miscellaneous information) for the period 1871-1880 and has published it. She is currently working on a similar project for the period 1861-1870.

A common occurrence, both in the Jewish and Gentile Communities, is of kinship marriage, which was perhaps made more necessary in small tight-knit communities anxious to preserve their cultural integrity. The shortage of marriage partners from without necessitated an inward-looking mentality which favoured cousin and even closer-type marriages. In Jewish Law, the prohibitions of consanguinity are not as rigid as those of England and, for example, a man could marry his niece. However, Jewish Law does not permit a woman to marry her nephew and the probable religious basis behind this is that the uncle/niece relationship is likely to be fertile but the aunt/nephew union might only take place after the aunt has become too old for childbearing. In Orthodox tradition, the encouragement for marriages to produce children is strong and contraception is prohibited. Furthermore, a widower could marry his deceased wife's sister, the so-called Levirate marriage, but such unions were not legal in England before 1921. If such a marriage did take place, it would have to be overseas, although the couple could then live legally in this country. Another Jewish tradition is that an unmarried man was actually expected to marry the widow of his deceased brother if the former union had not produced any children.

Marriages under the auspices of an Orthodox synagogue may only take place if it is clear that both bride and groom are themselves of Jewish parentage; that is, that the parents have themselves married under Orthodox Jewish Law. There are, of course, occasions when one or other party is a proselyte (that is converted to the Jewish faith) and unless the conversion is in accordance with Orthodox tradition, the validity of the marriage will be denied by the Orthodox authorities. It was anxieties of this nature from the Orthodox perspective, that led to the reluctance of the Orthodox Community to sanction conversions arranged under Reform or more progressive authorities. According to Rabbinic Law, Judaism descends through the mother, which means that in a mixed marriage, if the mother is herself Jewish then so are the children, but not so with the children of a Jewish father and a Gentile mother, unless the mother has herself previously converted under Orthodox auspices. It is difficult to be sure, in numerical terms, how many Jews may have deviated from the strict Orthodoxy of previous generations and have 'married out'. However, the existence of such a situation has been widespread for many centuries. Inevitably, if the numbers of potential marriageable partners are too few, notwithstanding inter-related marriages, the 'temptation' to practise exogamy is very strong.

From the genealogical point of view, apart from the civil certificates obtainable in the usual way, the most likely sources of information on Jewish marriages are from the well-established Jewish congregations under whose auspices marriages may well have occurred. The most senior of these congregations are London-based, in particular, the Bevis Marks Sephardi Congregation dating from the late-17th century. Some important collections of marriages, such as those of the Bevis Marks Congregation, have been published at least as far as the beginning of the 20th century and are held by the Society of Genealogists. For further details it will be necessary to approach the religious authorities of the particular Congregation concerned, and there may be more details available than in the secular certificates procedure. Regrettably there is no consolidated list of all the published Jewish congregational records. Many provincial congregations have accepted the authority of the United Synagogue, and the religious documentation for their marriages will, therefore, be retained in the Archive Office of the Chief Rabbi. These records are not published but can be consulted by the archivist. Some of the background information sometimes available (particularly from 1880) includes details of the date and place of birth of the parties (if they had been born abroad), evidence of Jewish status and names of siblings of the groom.

Although this chapter is essentially about marriage, its corollary (divorce) requires some consideration. In Orthodox Jewish practice, if a Jewish couple divorced, the husband had to give a 'get' (a religious document of divorce) to his wife before she was allowed to marry again under Jewish religious authority. This system of Jewish divorce differs from most other divorce procedures in that it is only an act of the divorcing parties to the marriage. No court or other official is involved, as such. Until 1866, the London authorities supervised the distribution of 'gettim' but by then the Registrar General was no longer prepared to accept such an arrangement as valid under English Law. Thereafter, a 'get' could only be issued at the same time as or after a secular court had granted the decree absolute. The involvement of the state in hitherto Jewish autonomous practice inevitably gave rise to irregular divorces, 'stille gettim', analogous with 'stille chuppah'. Around the end of the last century, numerous foreign-born Rabbis, by then living in England, were ready to help their co-religionists by granting religious divorces, albeit unacceptable in English Law. It is possible that, on occasion, people held the erroneous view that where a marriage had taken place abroad, an English civil divorce was, therefore, unnecessary. However, the costs of involving the civil system were usually prohibitive, as even conceded by Chief Rabbi Doctor Herman Adler when he gave evidence before the Royal Commission on Divorce and Marital Causes in December 1910.[5]

Illustration 1

Illustration 1 & 1a
Ketubah (marriage contract) of Harry Muscovitch and Janet Lachinsky, otherwise Janet Myers, 30 December 1915, New Road Synagogue, London. Reproduced from the family papers, with the permission of Ms Helene Howard (granddaughter).

14

ABSTRACT OF THE כתובה

On the *5th* day of the week, the *23rd*
day of the month *Tebeth*, in the year 567*6* A.M.,
corresponding to the *30th* of *December* 191*5*
the holy Covenant of Marriage was entered into in London,
between the Bridegroom—

Harry Muscovitch

and his Bride— *Janet Lachinsky*
otherwise
Janet Myers

The said Bridegroom made the following declaration to his
Bride :

" Be thou my wife according to the Law of Moses and
of Israel. . I faithfully promise that I will be a true husband
unto thee I will honour and cherish thee ; I will work for
thee ; I will protect and support thee, and will provide all
that is necessary for thy due sustenance, even as it beseemeth a
Jewish husband to do I also take upon myself all such further
obligations for thy maintenance, during thy lifetime, as are
prescribed by our religious statute."

And the said Bride has plighted her troth unto him, in
affection and in sincerity, and has thus taken upon herself
the fulfilment of all the duties incumbent upon a Jewish wife.

This Covenant of Marriage was duly executed witnessed
this day, according to the usage of Israel.

Illustration 1a

15

CHAPTER 5: DEATHS AND BURIALS

The importance of necrology as a genealogical source is, of course, very well-known. The rules concerning Jewish burials are mostly concerned with the religious preparation of the body very soon after death and rapid interment (a maximum of three days between death and burial is traditional). Frequently a death will occur in the morning and the burial will take place that afternoon. In Jewish tradition, the tombstone should be erected within a period of one year from death, and a relatively modern custom (about two hundred years or so) is to have a ceremony of 'setting' the memorial stone. In very Orthodox tradition, the children of the deceased should not be named on the stone, which is a genealogical disadvantage. However, frequently the custom is ignored and the inscriptions can be very useful.[6] An example from the Cheltenham Jewish Burial Ground reads 'In memory of Hannah Myer, widow of the late Abraham Myer. Born Great Yarmouth 7th August 1815, died 9th February 1902 and buried at Willesden'. Others in the Burial Ground had been born in Jamaica, while another inscription in the same cemetery, relating to a person born in 1825 in Russia and dying in Cheltenham in 1863, carried the additional text: 'Here rests in God far from his country'.

If the burial ground is still in use, the information may be obtained from the cemetery superintendent, but if the cemetery is defunct, it may only be possible to visit it by arrangement. Inscriptions from numerous Jewish burial grounds have been transcribed and indexed, and publications featuring burial registers kept by Jewish Congregations can also be very helpful, such as that of the Bevis Marks Congregation from 1733-1918. A partial transcription of the old (now closed) Jewish Burial Ground in Falmouth was published in the *Jewish Chronicle* in 1910. A major transcription of the Bristol Jewish Cemeteries is also available[7] and a partial listing of the interments in the old (now closed) Jewish Burial Ground in Birmingham was published in the *Birmingham Jewish Recorder* in July 1955.

Many death notices, obituaries and similar data have been published both in the *Jewish Chronicle* and in numerous secular newspapers. For the most part these are available at the Newspaper Library in Colindale. A set of the *Jewish Chronicle* is also available at University College, London, and a further full set exists at the Birmingham Office of the International Jewish Genealogical Resources (IJGR), whose address is given in a later section of this book. Access to this latter set may be granted by direct arrangement with the IJGR.

The Jewish Year begins in September or October and is 3760 years ahead of the secular dating system. Therefore, an event in (say) 5700 (Jewish Year) will have taken place between September/October 1940 and September/October 1941. *The Jewish Year*

Book and other almanacs frequently give comparative tables between the Jewish and secular calendars. *The Jewish Year Book*, published by the *Jewish Chronicle*, has been produced annually since 1896. It is available via the *Jewish Chronicle* or frequently, sets exist in various public libraries, but it is a matter of chance as to whether they can be located in a particular area.

During the seven days immediately after a person's death, the next-of-kin 'sit shivah'. This 'week of mourning' is an important religious obligation, and frequently a subsequent notice from the immediate relatives of a deceased might appear in a Jewish newspaper, thanking those who have shown sympathy to them during this period of time. These notices can be genealogically extremely valuable in that many siblings, children or other close relatives might make the same announcement and also list their own addresses and relationships. This may help discover information about the married names of daughters or sisters and the existence of other siblings or sons hitherto unsuspected.

The *Jewish Chronicle* frequently reported the deaths of Jews who had died abroad (possibly at the request of relatives living in the United Kingdom) and sometimes the announcement also suggests that foreign papers of a particular country should copy and report the notice of death. This may mean that there are relatives in that country who needed to be notified and will suggest that an investigation of the links the deceased had with that country might be useful. The *Gentleman's Magazine,* to which reference has been made on several occasions already, has also published many items concerning the death of Jews, and an indexed listing of these has been compiled under the title 'Jewish Obituaries in the *Gentleman's Magazine* 1731-1868' which was published in the *Miscellanies* Part IV of the Jewish Historical Society of England in 1942.

One important point concerning the memorial stones erected to deceased Jews is the interaction between Hebrew and English. Nearly all Jewish tombstones will be written, at least partly, if not completely, in Hebrew and the dates of the deceased person will be given in accordance with the Hebrew calendar. Since the Jewish naming custom refers to the son or daughter of the father, the Hebrew name will reveal, at least, the name of the father of the deceased, for example Moses son of Abraham or Sarah daughter of Abraham, etc. If the deceased was of the priestly (Cohen) or sub-priestly (Levi) tribes then the tombstone will state as such: Moses ben Abraham Ha-Cohen or Sarah bas Abraham Ha-Levi. There are also frequently traditional Hebrew formulas on the stones, for men or for women, including exhortations that the soul may be bound up in the bundle of eternal life. These are simply traditional religious benedictions and of no genealogical value.

CHAPTER 6
CENSUS RETURNS, NATURALISATION
AND DENIZATION RECORDS

The decennial Census has been taken in Britain regularly since 1801 with the exception of 1941. However, names from returns for 1801-1831 inclusive have not survived, so the first of these sources of any genealogical value is the 1841 version. No relationship to the head of the house is described in this Census and the ages are rounded down to the nearest five years, apart from under 15 year-olds. A significant number of Jewish people living in Britain in 1841 had been born in various parts of Europe, but unfortunately the only listing for these is 'F' (i.e. foreign parts). The 1851 and subsequent censuses usually give a more specific country of birth and sometimes even the town or locality. This may be very valuable used in conjunction with a gazetteer, such as *Where Once We Walked*,[8] which is specifically focused on the Jewish Communities across a wide swathe of Eastern Europe. As is well-known, the 1881 Census, thanks to the efforts of so many volunteers from various genealogical societies, has been transcribed to provide a country-wide index for virtually every name. Unfortunately, due to problems with handwriting, enumerators' understanding of names given to them, etc., there have been some curious errors created. For instance, the name 'Steinberg' has sometimes emerged as 'Henbery'[9]. However, the advantages of being able to locate far-flung members of a family who appear unexpectedly in different parts of the realm, outweigh the disadvantages of the occasional mistranscription. By the time of the 1891 Census, certain parts of England (notably the East End of London) had such dense Jewish populations, many of whom were not at all well-versed in English, that the authorities sought help from Jewish institutions such as the Chief Rabbinate or the Board of Deputies. Where appropriate, the enumerators were empowered to offer the head of the household an opportunity of recording the information in Yiddish, Hebrew, Polish or Russian. The enumerator then received help from an appropriate translator to record the information in the vernacular.[10]

The words 'British Subject' may appear in a census return, which suggests that the person has undergone naturalisation (unless he came from Hanover, which was a British Protectorate, before 1837). However, the lack of such words does not automatically preclude naturalisation. The use of the words 'Naturalised British Subject' is virtually proof that naturalisation has taken place. Lists of naturalisation and denization papers are available at the Public Record Office at Kew in Class HO, but with the closure of the Chancery Lane Branch of the Public Record Office there is now no longer such a listing in Central London. The Huguenot Society has published indexes to naturalisations by private acts of Parliament up to 1800 in volumes 8, 18, 27 and 35 of its quarto series publications. The Jewish Historical Society of England published

'A list of Jewish persons endenizened & naturalized 1609-1799' in Part VII of the *Miscellanies* of the Jewish Historical Society of England. The Society of Genealogists holds these and microfilm copies of the indexes to naturalisations 1801-1924 and denizations 1801-1873.

The naturalisation papers themselves are available at Kew, subject to the restrictions of the privacy rules, but these may vary at the discretion of the officials. The information contained in the original papers is variable, but the minimum data given would be the length of time of residence in Britain, whether married or unmarried, occupation and country of origin, together with the names of the guarantors. Frequently information is given about the town within the country of origin, together with the various addresses at which the applicant has lived and often the numbers and names of his children. Sometimes an exact date of birth is provided, and also the names of the parents. However, since the information is frequently supplied only by the applicant it may, therefore, be subject to 'sanitisation' if the applicant preferred to present information in such a way. For example, Abraham Jackson, who was naturalised in Liverpool in 1919, told the authorities that he had been born in Talkutchkoo, Smolensk, Russia, on 17th December 1881. The Under-Secretary of State specifically enquired about his original name, to which he replied that 'my father bore the surname of Jackson before he left Russia but it was written in Russian script. When I went to night school in London to learn English my teacher asked me how I pronounced my name and wrote it down as Jackson. The nearest English equivalent to the Russian letters comprising my surname spelled Jackson and that is all I can remember as I left Russia when I was twelve years of age, twenty-six years ago.' The authorities must have been happy enough with this unlikely explanation, and his Certificate of Allegiance was duly granted. However, it is improbable in the extreme that 'Jackson' was, indeed, the original Russian or Yiddish name he received at birth.

An alternative to consulting the calendars of naturalisations themselves, although not as informative, is to look for a listing in the *London Gazette*. Such a listing may give the full address and occupation of the applicant at the time which is, therefore, at least one step forward.

The Aliens' Act of 1836 has given rise to 236 volumes of certificates of aliens recorded between 1836 and 1852. These are classified under the port of arrival and are in the Public Record Office (Class HO2). For background information on this and other acts for the registration of aliens see Kershaw and Pearsall, *Immigrants and aliens. A guide to sources on UK immigration and citizenship.*

CHAPTER 7: WILLS AND ADMINISTRATIONS

It has been claimed that the ambition of every Jew is to leave each of his sons no less a sum of money than had been left to him by his own father. Be that as it may, wills, letters of administration, grants, probates etc., leave valuable records for the genealogist and may, on occasion, vividly illuminate family politics. Where the testator has died is immaterial, but there would have to be assets in Britain requiring distribution, under the jurisdiction of an appropriate court. Since 1st January 1858 all grants have been administered through the Family Division of the High Court, and the Principal Registry is now based at First Avenue House, 42-49 High Holborn, London WC1V 6NP. Numerous copies of the calendars of grants are available in some local probate offices and libraries, but for grants prior to the creation of the centralised probate system, it may be much more complicated to discover their whereabouts. The most important pre-1858 repositories are the Prerogative Court of Canterbury[11] and the Prerogative Court of York, but many local consistory courts, usually loosely based on a county town, may need checking out. The Prerogative Court of Canterbury is the most important simply because it is the largest in the country and was the one most favoured for Jewish grants, probably because the greatest number of the community lived in or near London and it was, therefore, the most convenient court for them. For details of all the published indexes to wills and administrations in the PCC 1383-1800 see Jeremy Gibson's *Probate jurisdictions. Where to look for wills.*

In the case of first generation Jews who settled in this country, their testamentary dispositions might frequently leave legacies to brothers, sisters or other relatives in their countries of origin. An example would be an ancestor of mine, Jonas Lazarus, who lived in Lincoln for many years and died there in November 1851, appointed his executor as his friend, Joseph Greiffenhagen, and certified the document by what was allegedly 'his mark' – in fact it was clearly his own name, but written in Hebrew script. The will, proved at Lincoln, mentions two daughters and a grand-daughter but provides little other information about the family.

Another example, proved at the Consistory Court of Exeter in 1792, is the administration of Barnet Levy of Falmouth. It reads 'Whereas Barnet Levy of Falmouth, County Cornwall, shopkeeper deceased, died intestate and administration of his goods was committed to Levy Levy, his son, and whereas the said Levy Levy did for some time intermeddle in the effects of his father and he is since dead intestate, leaving some part thereof unadministered, the Vicar General now empowers certain clerks to take oaths of Betsy Levy, Hannah Levy and Judith Levy, spinsters, the three daughters of the next-of-kin of the said Barnet Levy.' It is particularly fortunate to have this copy of the document since the original was destroyed in 1941 when Exeter was blitzed and the local repository was severely damaged.

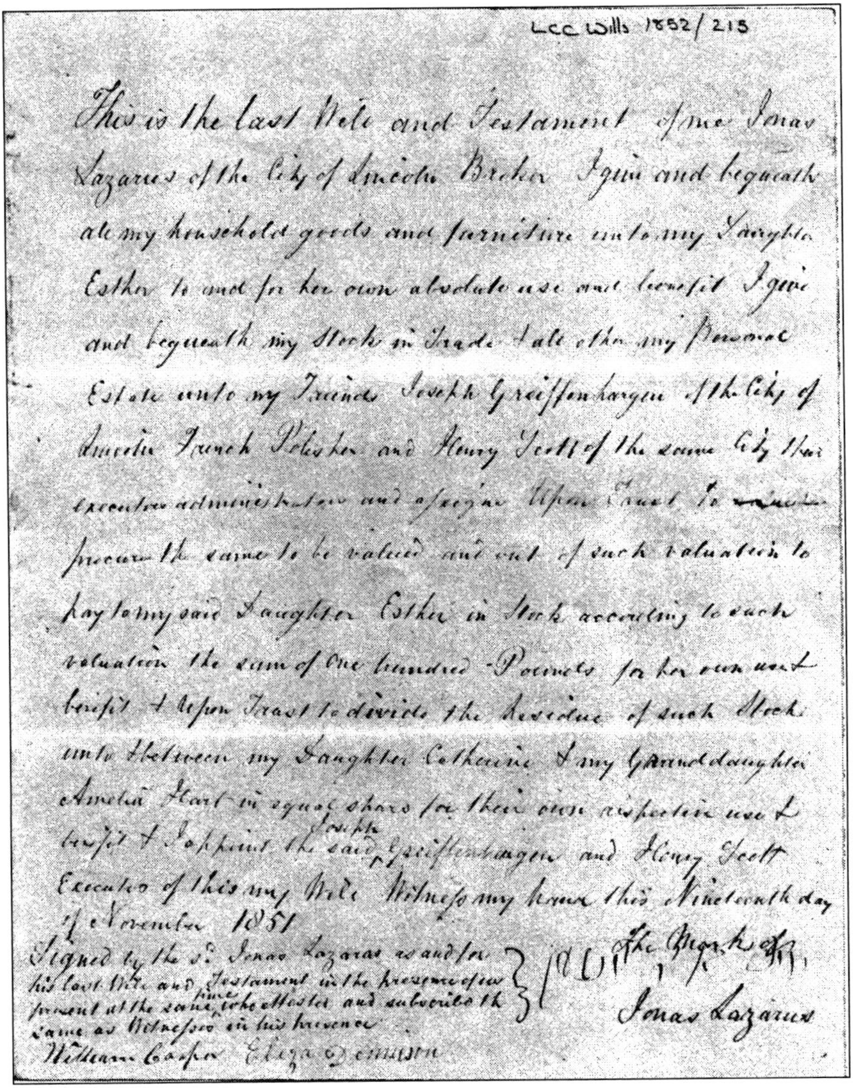
LCC Wills 1852/215

This is the last Will and Testament of me Jonas Lazarus of the City of Lincoln Broker I give and bequeath all my household goods and furniture unto my Daughter Esther to and for her own absolute use and benefit I give and bequeath my Stock in Trade & all other my Personal Estate unto my Friends Joseph Greiffenhagen of the City of Lincoln French Polisher and Henry Scott of the same City their executors administrators and assigns Upon Trust to procure the same to be valued and out of such valuation to pay to my said Daughter Esther in Stock according to such valuation the sum of One hundred Pounds for her own use & benefit & upon Trust to divide the Residue of such Stock unto & between my Daughter Catherine & my Granddaughter Amelia Hart in equal shares for their own respective use & benefit & I appoint the said Joseph Greiffenhagen and Henry Scott Executors of this my Will Witness my hand this Nineteenth day of November 1851

Signed by the sd Jonas Lazarus as and for his last Will and Testament in the presence of us present at the same time who attested and subscribed the same as Witnesses in his presence

William Casper Eliza Dennison

The Mark of Jonas Lazarus

Illustration 2

Will of Jonas Lazarus of the City of Lincoln. Reproduced with the permission of Lincolnshire Record Office LCC wills 1852/215.

Another example of a will rich in background information, is 'Will of Bernard S. proved by PCC 1831. Dated 8 May 1830. Of Kingston, Jamaica and about to leave the island for his health. Sons – Bernard and Philip San J. alias James S. Sister – Malchen wife of David L. of Germany who has a large family. Sisters – Julia, Judith, Yetchen, Sanchen, and Jane, all of Germany. Brothers – Sigismund and Samuel of London. Brother-in-law – Solomon C. Codicil, dated 19 August 1830. Signed in Frankfurt. About to marry Miss Adelade L. daughter of his beloved sister. He reduced the legacy to Bernard (son born in Kingston, Jamaica on 5 September 1825) and also reduced the legacy to James Philippe (born in ? on 1 May 1828). Codicil, dated 6 October 1830. Signed in Frankfurt. Date of Bernard's death corrected to 1824. Also testator stated that he was not married to the mother of his sons. Proved March 1831 by Samuel S of London – Sigismund then being in Jamaica.' Perhaps also of interest, his son Bernard died intestate in Baltimore, Maryland, United States of America. He was a bachelor and a bastard. The estate was valued at £1,000 and letters of administration were granted to a nominee of Her Majesty for the benefit and use of Her Majesty.

CHAPTER 8
OTHER SECULAR RECORDS AND THEIR
JEWISH IMPLICATIONS

As has been seen from the previous chapters, there are numerous secular archival sources or even the records of other ethnic groupings, that it may be appropriate to consult even in researching Jewish family lines. For example, street and town directories, professional directories, school registers, the records of municipal cemeteries, private printed pedigrees, general newspapers, court reports, rate books and public documentation (such as land ownership) may all, on occasion, yield useful data. Of course, these sources will deal primarily with the largely non-Jewish population and there is often no specific way in which the individuals named in some of these sources may be known as being Jewish. However, from time to time the secular or even the specific ethnic (non-Jewish) listing may clearly identify its Jewish reference point. For example, some of the early parish registers explain their listing of Jewish births at the express request of the parents, although not involving baptism.[3] This was presumably because the parish registers at the time were the only means available for recording specific primary events. The International Genealogical Index (IGI) certainly has many references, especially in the 'Jewish' areas, such as the East End of London, (part of Middlesex), to names that are at least suggestive of Jewish origin. Clearly, if baptism has occurred it may be as a result of conversion to Christianity.

School registers, both of general secular schools and specific Jewish schools, may have been deposited with the local authority archive and, as with street or town directories, may provide addresses for checking through the censuses.

Many municipal cemeteries may have Jewish people buried within them or even have a specific Jewish section, and such documentation again may have been deposited with the local archive.

Rate books do not specifically yield Jewish data, but by inference from the names and especially if they are clustered in an area where it is known that Jews favoured, it may be a reasonable deduction that a Jewish family has been located.

The national newspapers and the local provincial press may yield information concerning Jews and Jewish families. The Newspaper Library in Colindale has a major collection of all these periodicals and also of the *Jewish Chronicle* and *Voice of Jacob* which are the most important early such relevant ethnic publications. They start in 1841. The *Voice of Jacob* was a short-lived Jewish newspaper, a precursor and contemporary of the *Jewish Chronicle*, but it folded after a few months.

An example from the provincial press, taken from the *Lincolnshire, Stamford and Rutland Mercury* of 13th April 1832, states '[DIED] On Sunday night, under circumstances of great worldly depression, Mrs Lazarus, wife of Jonas Lazarus, of this city. It is earnestly hoped that the distressed and destitute condition of this numerous Jewish family, and especially the helpless infants who are so early deprived of a mother's care, will engage the sympathy of the benevolent ladies and gentlemen of the town and neighbourhood' (See also Chapter 5).

The *Gentleman's Magazine* which appears from the mid-18th century to the early-20th century, frequently published items of Jewish interest. The genealogical value of the material varies enormously, but colourful accounts of Jewish ceremonies, such as weddings, seemed to have been matters of interest to the *Magazine's* reading public.

CHAPTER 9: SURNAMES

Although in biblical times Jewish names may have arisen from a variety of religious traditions, the transmutation of these ideas into modern times has been influenced by many accretions from numerous different cultures. The essential concept is that a person is a son or daughter of their father and a tribal or other religious addition may be subsumed in the name. For example, Abraham ben Moses or Abraham ben Moses Ha-Cohen (of the priestly line). Sometimes nicknames and other sobriquets have been attached to numerous dynasties, for example, Katzenellenbogen ('cat's elbows') refers to one very illustrious tribe.

The essential simplicity of the Jewish naming system was perhaps inadequate with the development of modern society, but it survived more or less unchanged until Napoleonic times. At this point various decrees in different parts of Europe insisted on the adoption of surnames. Several different mechanisms have then operated to produce the present-day names. The straightforward taking of biblical (patriarchal) names such as Abraham(s), Isaac(s), Jacob(s) or Moses, etc. occurred commonly. Similarly, many Jews became Cohen, Levy, Israel, etc. However, trade names, occupation names, place names, colour names and more esoteric derivations were also widely employed. All these systems have been expressed in numerous languages such as German, Russian, Polish, Yiddish, Dutch, Italian or Spanish and Portuguese. When the immigrant Jew arrived in England he may have retained one or other of these names acquired by whatever technique may have applied in his case, or he may then have anglicised it! In that process, numerous different spellings may have arisen and different members of the same family may have applied the ideas inconsistently, so that brothers may have ended up with apparently very different names. For example, Grunberg or Monteverdi might translate/transliterate as (abbreviated) Green or Greenberg or Greenhill. So many permutations are possible that it is difficult to predict from any given name its specific origin. If the derivation is known it usually becomes clear, but deducing it without the benefit of post-event knowledge requires considerable imagination.

As if the topic is not confused enough already, sometimes additional names arose more or less by choice. For example, Benjamin ben David might end up as Benjamin David or Benjamin Davis. In the will of Samson Lucas it refers to his brother, Moses Levy *Newton*, and it appears that the surname was adopted because Moses Levy took it from the name of a business partner. The Dutch family of Groomsfeld assumed the surname of Jones when Isaiah Groomsfeld, arriving in Great Yarmouth, saw the name over a shop, and thought it more pronounceable than his own. It is more than possible that mythology and embellishment surrounds many of the naming traditions, but variety exists in profusion. It is certainly known that Isaac Moses of Ipswich had three sons who became respectively Marsden, Moss and Merton. Subsequently some of the descendants of this last tribe took the surname of Beddington, this being the Surrey village in which they settled.

A man sometimes took the maiden name of his wife in lieu of his own surname and more rarely, it would seem, that of his mother-in-law. Benjamin Levi, an engraver from Wiesbaden, settled in Portsmouth around 1740. One of his grandsons, Solomon Jacob Levi, married Rachael Hort. Rachael was the daughter of Nahuem Hort and his wife, Jane Waley. Nahuem was the son of Abraham Hort, otherwise Abraham Kampen, and Jane was the daughter of Samuel Waley, the latter having changed his name from Wheli to Waley, himself being the son of Rabbi Aaron Wheli of Prague. Solomon Jacob Levi decided to assume the maiden name of his mother-in-law, Jane and so became Solomon Jacob Waley. Later still there was a marriage between Solomon Jacob Waley's granddaughter, Julia Mathilda Waley and Nathanial Louis Cohen and this brought into existence the surname Waley-Cohen.

There is no easy way of following the many changes of these surnames, except that they have been recorded, as is the case of some of the better-known families. There is no central registry of changes of names and, indeed, few will be recorded formally. Some records are held at the Public Record Office which publishes a useful information leaflet *Legal Records Information no. 32: Changes of Name*

The matter is further complicated by Welsh and Cornish use of biblical patronymic names (such as Joseph, Isaac or Abraham) which are merely respectful of Jewish tradition but do not mean that the Welsh or Cornish people are themselves Jewish.

CHAPTER 10: FORENAMES

If it is complicated to discover the origin and background of a so-called Jewish surname, the matter is no simpler when dealing with forenames.

It used to be the custom amongst the Ashkenazim that a child was not named after a living ancestor and if, therefore, he appeared to have the same name as his father, the suggestion is he would have been born posthumously. The Ashkenazim felt superstitious about naming people after the living and thought it might shorten their lives. This is not the case for the Sephardim, where naming after a living relative (usually a grandparent) is considered a form of honouring that person. After emancipation and while retaining their original name for religious purposes, Jews often used a secular version, such as Elizabeth for Billa, Fanny for Faigel, etc. In Ashkenazi tradition, providing the grandparents are dead, the first son is given the name of the paternal grandfather and the second that of the maternal grandfather.[12]

Jewish males are circumcised at the age of eight days and the circumcision records are the nearest equivalent, from the genealogical point-of-view, to the Christian baptism. However, unlike Christian records of baptisms, which are the property of the churches, the circumcision registers did not belong to the synagogues but were the property of the individual circumciser (called a mohel) who undertook the procedure. Sometimes registers have survived in the private papers of the descendants of the practitioners and sometimes they have been placed in such repositories as the Jewish Museum or even with a local synagogue or local authority. The coverage period is nothing like as extensive as the baptismal records of the churches. Such circumcision registers as are extant and have been deposited may also be of very variable value, since they do not necessarily include surnames but may only have the Hebrew or synagogal names used in Jewish ritual procedures. They may be written in a variety of languages such as Hebrew, Yiddish, Ladino or other vernacular, but one or two very valuable examples, such as the De Paiba register from 1715-1758 of the Bevis Marks Synagogue, are available. This latter has been transliterated and translated by the Sephardi authorities and is in the public domain. It is of particular interest in that it covers about 1,500 cases, by no means exclusively Sephardi, and refers to circumcisions carried out in many parts of England, not just simply London. Of course, the circumcision registers, where they are available, refer only to male cases!

It will be noted from all this that discovering details of Jewish births prior to 1837 (the date of civil registration) may be difficult, if not impossible. A few synagogues, notably the Bevis Marks Congregation, as already mentioned, have retained lists of births, etc. registered with them, and these are now published. It has also been mentioned in a previous chapter that some Jews felt it disadvantageous not to have an official record of a birth, and so arranged for these details to be included in the Church of England parish records for the local parish within which they were born. Many of the City of London churches have such entries in their registers, frequently stating 'child of a Jew'.[3]

The Bar (or Bat)mitzva ceremony is usually held at a synagogue at around the time of the Jewish child's thirteenth birthday. In the case of the boy (Barmitzva) it marks the point at which he is considered to have achieved the status of manhood and can fulfil Jewish religious responsibilities. It is not a sacramental ritual and is relatively modern (since the 14th century), but for the past century or so parents have sometimes announced the event in the *Jewish Chronicle* or other equivalent newspaper. Much more rarely are announcements made for the girls' batmitzvat.

The secular equivalent of biblical-type names may not translate or transliterate exactly and this is sometimes a source of confusion. For example, in census returns you may find Jewish children apparently having names such as 'Christopher' or 'Mary'. These are certainly not usual in Jewish tradition. However, the explanation may be that the non-Jewish enumerator is more familiar with Mary than Miriam or Christopher than Kerpel (another version of Jacob).[13]

CHAPTER 11
LONDON AND OTHER COMMUNITIES

It was noted in the introductory chapter that although London has always been the home of the greater number of the Anglo-Jewish Community, many other congregations have existed and continue to flourish in numerous provincial towns. London itself is not homogeneous and has contained (and still does) many Jewish groupings scattered over the greater metropolis. Most of these congregations, while retaining considerable autonomy for their particular area, have maintained traditional links with one or other of the London-based senior religious institutions, such as the United Synagogue or the Sephardi Congregation. The *Jewish Year Book* published by the *Jewish Chronicle* since 1896, lists most of these congregations with abbreviated histories and an indication of the numbers of Jews still living in the region. By accessing *Jewish Year Books* over the past century or so, it is possible to follow the fluctuations (even including the demise in relevant cases) of Jewish Communities over time. It may give guidance as to whether records appertaining to specific individuals will be found in a given region. Peter Renton has also published a guide to the lost synagogues of London.

Cecil Roth gave a series of lectures on various provincial Jewish communities and these have been gathered together and published under the title *The Rise of Provincial Jewry*.[14] As so many provincial communities retain their records themselves, Roth's work, fifty years down the track, still remains the most valuable listing available. There have also been many individual histories of many Jewish communities and congregations, and the growth in the production of these histories is proceeding apace. Any such listing of these histories is inevitably going to be incomplete within a very short time of the publication of this booklet, due to the continued advances in this field. However, an important general source is that of the various publications of the Jewish Historical Society of England, mostly the *Transactions, Miscellanies and Historical Studies*. Amongst these volumes (about fifty so far published since the foundation of the Society in 1893) many stories of individual congregations will be found (some still extant and some defunct) with important bibliographies and references. All titles are listed in Mullins' *Texts and Calendars: an analytical guide to serial publications*. Notable amongst the Society's publications is its four volumes of bibliography starting with *Magna Anglo-Judaica Bibliotheca* and *Nova Anglo-Judaica Bibliotheca* with periodic updates. Biographical works include *Anglo-Jewish notabilities; their arms & testamentary dispositions* which contains the plan of a dictionary of Anglo-Jewish biography by Albert M Hyamson; *Anglo-Jewish coats of arms* by A Rubens; *Anglo-Jewish wills & letters of administration 1384-1840* by A P Arnold. A recent supplement to this work has been produced by Michael Jolles as *A Directory of Distinguished British Jews 1830-1930*.

CHAPTER 12: RESEARCH ABROAD
(with acknowledgement to Mr Michael Gandy, BA, FSG)

It is only a small number of contemporary English Jews who can trace their Jewish ancestry back in England earlier than the mid-19th century. Almost the whole of the present-day English Community stems from immigrants who arrived here from one of the countries of mainland Europe. Many people assume that the records will now more or less stop at that point. However, this is not necessarily the case. With careful research (and, it must be admitted, some luck) it may be possible to trace these Jewish lines of ancestry for a number of generations prior to the arrival of immigrants in the United Kingdom.

It is not usually adequate simply to know the country from whence the ancestor hailed. Due to lack of centralisation of records in many European lands, a more exact location, preferably a village itself, is necessary.

Family documents and family memories may give a clue, although different members of the same family may remember different versions of their family origins. Not many immigrants brought documentation with them. After settling in England, they may have tried to obtain evidence of marriage or birth, and the latter certificates were particularly needed at the start of the First World War when many Jews needed to prove whether they were born under Russian rule (thereby technically allies) or under German/Austrian rule (which made them technically enemy aliens). Most of the documents, where they have survived, will probably be written in a non-English language which may need translating. However, they are likely to contain a vital clue 'born at ......'. Sometimes the non-registration of a person actually born in England required a legal deposition to prove to the Home Secretary that the person was not an Enemy Alien. An example found amongst family papers is that of Goodman Aronson, born in Wolverhampton in 1860 but threatened with deportation in 1914 to his 'native' country which he had never visited in his life! The affidavits from his English-born relatives submitted to the Home Secretary, give much information about Aronson's immediate family background. However, tracking down such papers can be immensely difficult unless, for example, they survive with naturalisation documentation that has moved to the Public Record Office.

Naturalisations are an important source which have been discussed already in a previous chapter.

Shipping and Passenger Lists can be very helpful if they can be discovered. The problem is that they are non-existent before 1878 and fragmentary for some twenty years or so after then. They are un-indexed, so without knowing either the name of the ship, the port of arrival or embarkation, or the date of sailing, it is extremely difficult to research through this source. The Public Record Office publishes an information leaflet *Domestic Records Information 56: Ships Passenger Lists 1878-1960.*

The Landesmannschaften (that is, societies of immigrant Jews from the same district or city, etc.) provide information on the networking between relatives and friends who were already established in England or the USA and were trying to help their brethren arrive here. If a Landesmannschaften document indicates a person or people belonged to it, this provides a clue to the place of origin. On occasion, whole communities emigrated more or less at the same time, so that a general reading of the history of that community provides much background information as to the place of origin. It can be difficult to find details of a Landesmannschaften and it is more or less by word of mouth that such have existed. (Emeritus) Professor Aubrey Newman of the University of Leicester has undertaken research in this area. A notable example in this context is the Jewish Community of Sunderland that arrived *en masse* from Krottingen in 1881 and 1882.[14]

Within the past ten to fifteen years, numerous Jewish Genealogical Societies have been established in France, Switzerland, Holland and other countries, and their publications have regularly recorded an increasing quantity of data concerning their Jewish citizenry. If it is known that family background reached into one of these countries, by contacting the relevant genealogical society considerable progress is usually possible through the types of record that exist in those countries. There are such groupings as the Anglo-French Society or the Anglo-German Society which, though secular and not specifically Jewish, often have expertise concerning Jewish backgrounds. It is appropriate, when writing to these sorts of organisation, to enclose either a self-addressed envelope or reply-paid postage coupons, or to obtain appropriate denomination stamps from the relevant country and attach these to the letter.

For countries in Central and Eastern Europe, far more material has survived and has recently come to light than might have been imagined even only ten years ago. The popular impression that because of the persecution in Germany and countries overrun by Germany, most of the records must have been destroyed, is not necessarily the case. Furthermore, many towns in Eastern Europe are now becoming very aware of the value of their heritage and the desire by people in the West to learn more about their backgrounds. This has led to the establishment of numerous archivists and researchers in many of the towns and cities in Eastern Europe who are prepared to assist enquirers. Their command of English is variable and the fee rates for the work they undertake need to be established clearly in advance. The Nazi-inspired so-called 'Final Solution' was by no means an act of mindless vandalism, but a government-led plan with full administrative back-up. This means that many records exist and have been made available today. For that matter, the secular records for particular towns, while by no means only listing the Jewish inhabitants, should contain records of births, marriages and deaths in many instances. Although, of course, many cemeteries and gravestones were desecrated and vandalised during the Nazi period and afterwards in lands under Communist rule, much has also survived. The tombstone inscriptions, usually both in Hebrew and also in the language of country of origin, are valuable, although each may need to be translated. The Hebrew inscription, of course, is very likely to give an indication of the deceased's father's name as is customary with Jewish tombstones.

An interesting source are the Yizkor or Memorial books, often written by ordinary people about the communities they came from before they were annihilated during the Second World War. Many of these books may have been taken by individuals who survived or may have been left behind in archive offices. Some of these records have also found their way, by various routes, to Israel.

The State of Israel was established in 1948, and the 'Gathering In' of so many of the remnants of the almost-destroyed European Jewish Communities has led to an upsurge in Israeli interest in piecing together records of these vanished entities. Moreover, numerous much more recent migrations to Israel of Jews from many other lands such as several of the Russian Republics, Ethiopia and Iraq have led to a parallel upsurge of interest in the backgrounds of the Jews of these countries. Probably the most useful initial contact points are the Beth Hatefutsoth, the Israeli Genealogical Society and the Jewish Agency (for addresses see List of Repositories, etc). Yad Vashem (the Holocaust Martyrs and Heroes Remembrance Authority) is attempting to collect information on all six million Jews who perished at the hands of the Nazis. They list 'A page of testimony' about each person and the pages vary enormously in the quantity of information recorded. Recently some four million such names have been computerised at Yad Vashem and details can be supplied by the authorities at that Memorial Site. Other important repositories are the Central Archives for the History of the Jewish People in Jerusalem and the Jewish National and University Library. As with corresponding with other overseas societies or libraries, it is appropriate to enclose a self-addressed envelope and the reply-paid coupons.

The migration of Jewish people, as mentioned in the introductory chapter in this book, may mean that many other countries will have useful archives or resource information. The countries of the English-speaking world (the USA, Canada, South Africa, New Zealand and Australia) have all received substantial numbers of Jewish migrants and both the Jewish communal records and secular archival sources of these countries can all provide useful information for genealogical research. For that matter, large Jewish Communities have existed and do exist in various countries in South

America (Brazil, Argentina, Chile etc.) and probably the best initial contact points for many of these countries may be determined by reference to the listings of their Communal offices in the *Jewish Year Book*.

The First International Jewish Genealogical Seminar was held in Jerusalem in 1984, and amongst the many important Jewish genealogical impetuses that arose out of that gathering was the creating of AVOTAYNU. This organisation now publishes a regular scholarly journal with contact points world-wide and details of the International Association of Jewish Genealogical Societies. Avotaynu itself is a member of this umbrella international society, as are also most of the other Jewish Genealogical Societies worldwide.

No genealogical advisory book can be complete without a mention of the work of the Church of Latter-Day Saints of Jesus Christ (the Mormons). Their contribution to record preservation, making such records available and encouraging enthusiasm for genealogical research, is unparalleled and very well-known. There is, of course, a theological motive behind the Mormon interest in genealogy but such matters are beyond the scope of this book. On occasions, there have been tensions between owners of important Jewish registers and the Mormon community, but for the most part the Church has behaved in a non-theological 'neutral' manner and it has not attempted to use its position as a genealogical authority to proselytise amongst seekers of information. The Church has been particularly impressive in its micro-filming of so many of the original registers (many of which it was thought had not survived) from vanished Jewish Communities of Central and Eastern Europe. Much of this material has now been transcribed and indexed, and copies of the original micro-films can be made available at many of the Church Family History Centres. Ideally, visiting Salt Lake City (the central repository of the Church) would offer the best opportunity for total genealogical researching on any one site anywhere in the world. It is not necessary to adhere to the Mormon faith to be allowed access to all the genealogical information contained in Salt Lake City.

NOTES

1. Abramson, Glenda, *The Blackwell Companion to Jewish Culture* (1989) pp 260/261.

2. Newman, Professor Aubrey, *The Records of the Poor Jews' Temporary Shelter* (held c/o, Department of History, University of Leicester).

3. Steel, D J (and Edgar R Samuel), *National Index of Parish Registers Volume 3: Sources for Roman Catholic and Jewish Genealogy and Family History* (Society of Genealogists, 1974) pp 957-976.

4. George Rigal – personal communication.

5. Tucker, Charles, 'Jewish Marriages and Divorces in England until 1940' Part 1 in *Genealogists' Magazine* Volume 24 No. 3 September 1992 pp 87-92, and Volume 24 No. 4 December 1992 pp 139-143.

6. Susser, Rabbi Doctor Bernard, *How to read and Record a Jewish Tombstone* (1995).

7. Tobias, Alan and Sheila, Judith Samuel, Audrey Greenwood, Marlene Sutton, Rabbi Hilel Simon, Sam Silverman, Sam Wirenberg and Michael Hill, *A Catalogue of the Burials in the Jewish Cemeteries of Bristol* (1997).

8. Mokotoff, Gary and Sally Ann Amdur Sack, *Where Once We Walked* (1991).

9. David, Gompertz - personal communication.

10. Newman, Professor Aubrey and Diana Rau, *1891 Census – Index of Heads of Family* (1994).

11. Arnold, Arthur P, 'Anglo-Jewish Wills and Letters of Administration relating to the Prerogative Court of Canterbury' (reprinted from *Anglo-Jewish Notabilities* 1949).

12. Samuel, Edgar R, *New Light on the Selection of Jewish Children's Names* Volume 23 of *Transactions of the Jewish Historical Society of England* (1971).

13. Gorr, Rabbi Shmuel and Chaim Freedman, *Jewish Personal Names*, (1992).

14. Roth, Cecil, *The Rise of Provincial Jewry*, 1950.

BIBLIOGRAPHY

Alderman, Geoffrey, *Modern Anglo-Jewry* (Oxford, Clarendon Press, 1992)

Alderman, Geoffrey, *The Federation of Synagogues, 1887-1987* (London, Federation of Synagogues, 1987)

Andrade, Jacob APM, *Record of the Jews in Jamaica* (Jamaica, Jamaican Times Limited, 1941)

Barnett, Richard D and P Wright *The Jews of Jamaica: Tombstone Inscriptions 1663-1880* (Jerusalem, Ben Zvi Institute, 1997)

Beider, Alexander, *A Dictionary of Jewish Surnames from the Kingdom of Poland* (Teaneck, New Jersey, Avotaynu, 1996)

Beider, Alexander *A Dictionary of Jewish Surnames from the Russian Empire* (Teaneck, New Jersey, Avotaynu, 1993)

Benas, BL, 'Records of the Jews in Liverpool' in *Transactions of the Historical Society of Lancashire and Cheshire* (Volume 51, 1901)

Benas, BL, 'Later Records of the Jews in Liverpool' in *Transactions of the Historical Society of Lancashire and Cheshire* (Volume 80, 1929)

Berger, Doreen, *The Jewish Victorian (Genealogical Information from Jewish newspapers 1871-1880)* (London, 1999)

Bermant, Chaim, *The Cousinhood: The Anglo-Jewish Gentry* (London, Eyre and Spottiswood, 1971)

Birmingham, Stephen, *Our Crowd* (Macdonald and Co., Futura Publications, 1971)

Black, Doris, *The Plymouth Synagogue* (Typescript, 1961 Mocatta Pamphlets)

Abramson, Glenda, ed., *Blackwell Companion to Jewish Culture*, (Oxford, Blackwell, 1989).

Brook, Stephen, *The Club (The Jews of Modern Britain)* (London, Constable, 1989)

Cernery, Johni, 'Jewish American Research' in Eakle, A and J Cerney, *The Source: A Guidebook of American Genealogy* (Salt Lake City, Ancestry Publishing Company, 1984)

Clapsaddle, Carol, *Tracing your Jewish Roots in London: Personal Experience* (Jerusalem, The Society for the Jewish Family Heritage, Tel Aviv, 1988)

Collins, Kenneth E, *Second City Jewry: The Jews of Glasgow in the Age of Expansion 1790-1919* (Glasgow, Scottish Jewish Archives, 1990)

Dansky, Miriam, *Gateshead, Its Community, Its Personalities, Its Institutions* (Michigan, Targum Press, 1992)

Dietz, Alexander, *Stammbuch de Frankfurter Jüden 1348-1849* (English Edition, Camelford, Cornwall, Vanderher Publications, 1989)

Emden, Paul H, *Jews of Britain* (London, Sampson Low, Marston & Co., 1942)

Encyclopaedia Judaica (16 Vols, Jerusalem, Keter, 1971 and with Yearbooks)

Endelman, Todd M, *The Jews of Georgian England, 1714-1830: Tradition and Change in a Liberal Society* (Philadelphia, Jewish Publication Society of America, 1979)

35

Ettinger, Philip, *Hope Place in Liverpool Jewry 1836-1930* (T Lyon and Co., 1930)

Feldman, David, *Englishmen and Jews, Social Relations and Political Culture 1840-1914* (New Haven and London, Yale University Press, 1994)

Fisher, Nelson, *800 Years: The Story of Nottingham's Jews* (The History of Nottingham Jewry Research Team, 1998)

Freedman, Chaim, *Eliyahu's Branches: The Descendants of the Vilna Gaon and His Family* (Teaneck, New Jersey, Avotaynu, 1997)

Freedman, Murray, *1891 Census of Leeds: List of Jewish Residents* (Leeds, 1994)

Freedman, Murray, *Leeds Jewry: A History of Its Synagogues* (Leeds, 1995)

Freedman, Murray, *Leeds Jewry: The First Hundred Years* (Leeds, 1992)

Gartner, Lloyd P, *The Jewish Immigrant in England, 1870-1914* (London, Simon Publications, 1973)

Gibson, Jeremy, S W, *Probate Jurisdictions. Where to look for* (Federation of Family History Societies, 1997)

Goldberg, JW, *South Manchester Hebrew Congregation: Eighty Years of Progress 1872-1952*

Goldman, Hyman, *Short History of the Allerton, Liverpool, Hebrew Congregation* (T Lyon and Co., 1965)

Goldman, Lazarus Morris, *History of the Jews of New Zealand* (AH and AW Reed, Wellington, 1958)

Goldschmidt-Lehmann, *Anglo-Jewish Bibliography, 1971-1990* (London, J.H.S.E., 1992)

Green, Geoffrey L, *The Royal Navy and Anglo-Jewry 1740-1820* (London, 1989)

Greenbaum, Masha, *The Jews of Lithuania: A History of a Remarkable Community 1316-1945* (Jerusalem, 1995)

Harfield, G Eugene, *A Commercial Directory of the Jews of the United Kingdom* (Hewlett and Pierce, 1894)

Henriques, Henry Straus Quixano, *The Jews and The English Law* (Oxford, 1908 and Clifton, New Jersey, 1974)

Henriques, Ursula, *The Jews of South Wales: Historical Studies* (Cardiff, University of Wales Press, 1993)

Howitt, Arthur, *Richmond and its Jewish Connections* (Privately printed, 1930)

Hudaly, David, *Liverpool Old Hebrew Congregation 1780-1874* (Liverpool Old Hebrew Congregation, 1974)

Hyamson, Albert Montefiore, *The Sephardim of England: The Study of the Spanish and Portuguese Jewish Community 1490-1951* (1951, reprinted London, 1991)

Hyman, Louis, *The Jews of Ireland from Earliest Times to the Year 1910* (J.H.S.E. and Israel University Press, 1972)

Issroff, Saul in Wenzerul, Rosemary, ed. *Jewish Ancestors? A Beginner's Guide to Jewish Genealogy in Great Britain* (Jewish Genealogical Society of Great Britain, 2000)

Jacobs, Joseph and Wolf, Lucien, *Bibliotheca Anglo-Judaica: A Bibliographical Guide to Anglo-Jewish History* (London, publications of the Anglo-Jewish Historical Exhibition, 1888)

Jewish Encyclopaedia (12 Vols, New York, Funk and Wagnall, 1901-06)

Jewish Historical Society of England, *Miscellanies* (London, continuing series)

Jewish Historical Society of England, *Transactions* (London, continuing series)

The Jewish Year Book (London, since 1896, continuing series)

Jolles, Michael, *Chatham Hebrew Society synagogue ledger 1836-65* (London, 2000)

Jolles, Michael, *A Directory of Distinguished British Jews 1830-1930 with a selected compilation extending from 1830-2000* (London, 2001)

Jolles, Michael, *Samuel Isaac, Saul Isaac and Nathanial Isaacs* (London, 1998)

Jolles, Michael, *A Short History of the Jews of Southampton* (London, 1996)

Joseph, Anthony P and Judith Joseph, *Proceedings of the Second International Jewish Genealogical Seminar* (Birmingham, 1987)

Josephs, Zoe, *Birmingham Jewry, 1749-1914* (Birmingham Jewish Historical Research Group, 1980)

Josephs, Zoe, *Birmingham Jewry: More Aspects 1740-1930* (Birmingham Jewish Historical Research Group, 1984)

Kershaw, Roger & Mark Pearsall, *Immigrants and Aliens. A Guide to Sources in the UK on Immigration and Citizenship* (London, 2000)

Kraus, Ernest, *Leeds Jewry* (W Heffer & Son Limited, 1964)

Krausz, Armin, *Sheffield Jewry: Commentary on a Community* (Bar-Elan University Ramat-Gan, 1980)

Kurzweil, Arthur, *From Generation to Generation* (New York, 1977 and revised edition 1994)

Kurzweil, Arthur and Miriam Weiner, *The Encyclopaedia of Jewish Genealogy* Volume 1 sources in the United States and Canada (New Jersey, 1991)

Kushner, Tony, *A History of Jewish Archives in the United Kingdom* in Archives Volume 20 (1992)

Kushner, Tony, *The Jewish Heritage in British History: Englishmen and Jewishness* (London, Frank Cass 1992)

Lehmann, Ruth P, *Nova Bibliotheca Anglo-Judaica : A Bibliographical Guide to Anglo-Jewish History 1937-1960* (London J.H.S.E., 1961)

Lehmann, Ruth P, *Anglo-Jewish Bibliography 1937-1970* (London J.H.S.E. 1973)

Levi, John S and George FJ Bergman, *Australian Genesis : Jewish Convicts and Settlers 1788-1850* (Hale, 1974)

Levine, Harry, *Norwich Hebrew Congregation 1840-1980* (Mansfields Norwich Limited, 1961)

Levy, Arnold, *History of the Sunderland Jewish Community* (London, Macdonald, 1956)

Levy, Arnold, *The Story of the Gateshead Yeshivah* (Taunton, Wessex Press, 1952)

Levy, E Lawrence, *Birmingham Jewry (Then and Now) 1870-1919* (Birmingham, JG Hammond and Co 1919)

Lipman, Vivian David, *A Social History of the Jews in England 1850-1950* (London, Watts, 1954)

Lipman, Vivian David, *A History of the Jews in Britain since 1858* (Leicester and London University Press, 1990)

Lipman, Vivian David, *The Age of Emancipation 1815-1880 in Three Centuries of Anglo-Jewish History* (London, J.H.S.E., 1961)

Livshin, Rosalyn D, *The History of the Harrogate Jewish Community* (Leeds University Press, 1995)

Mokotoff, Gary and Sally Ann Amdur Sack, *Where Once We Walked* (Teaneck, New Jersey, Avotaynu, 1991)

Mosse, Werner E, *A Second Chance: Two Centuries of German-Speaking Jews in the United Kingdom* (Tubingen, J.C.B. Mohr, Paul Siebeck, 1991)

Mullins, E L C, *Texts and Calendars & Texts and Calendars II. An Analytical Guide to Serial Publications* (London, 1978 & 1983)

Naggar, Betty, *Jewish Peddlers and Hawkers, 1740-1940* (Camberley, Porphyrogenitus, 1992)

Nathan, E, *The History of the Jews in Singapore 1830-1945* (Singapore, 1986)

Newman, Aubrey, *The United Synagogue, 1870-1970* (London, Routledge and Kegan Paul, 1976)

Newman, Aubrey, *The Leicester Hebrew Congregation 1874-1974* (Leicester, 1974)

Olsover, L, *The Jewish Communities of North East England 1755-1980* (Gateshead, The Ashley Mark Publishing Co., 1981)

Oshry, Rabbi Ephraim, *The Annihilation of Lithuanian Jewry* (The Judaica Press, New York, 1995)

Pearce, Keith & Helens Fry eds., *Lost Jews of Cornwall from the middle ages to the 19th century,* (Bristol, Redcliff Press Ltd, 2000)

Pollins, Harold, *The Economic History of the Jews in England* (London, Associated University Presses Limited, 1982)

Renton, Peter, *The Lost Synagogues of London* (London, Tymsder Publishing, 2000)

Romain, Jonathan A and Anne J Kershen, *Tradition and Change: A History of Reform Judaism in Britain 1840-1995* (London, Valentine Mitchell, 1995)

Rosenstein, Neil, *The Unbroken Chain: Biographical Sketches and Genealogy of Illustrious Jewish Families from the 15th to the 20th Century* (New York, 1976) and revised enlarged version New York, 1990).

Rosenstein, Neil, *The Gaon of Vila and His Cousinhood* (New York, 1997)

Roth, Cecil, *A History of the Jews of England* (London, John Trotter Publishers, 1989)

Roth, Cecil, *The Rise of Provincial Jewry* (London, 1950)

Roth Cecil, *Magna Bibliotheca Anglo-Judaica: A Bibliographical Guide to Anglo-Jewish History* (London, J.H.S.E., 1937)

Rottenberg, Dan, *Finding Our Fathers: A Guidebook to Jewish Genealogy* (New York, Random House, 1977)

Samuel, Judith, *Jews in Bristol : A History of the Jewish Community in Bristol from the Middle Ages to the Present Day* (Bristol, Sansom and Company, 1997)

Samuel, Wilfred S, *Sources of Anglo-Jewish Genealogy* (London, Jewish Museum Publications, 1993)

Samuel, Wilfred S, *A Review of the Jewish Colonists in Barbados in the Year 1680* (London, J.H.S.E., 1936)

Shaw, William A, *Letters of Denization and Acts of Naturalisation for Aliens in England and Ireland, 1603-1700* Huguenot Society, Volume 18 (1911)

Shaw, William A, *Letters of Denization and Acts of Naturalisation for Aliens in England and Ireland, 1701-1800* Huguenot Society, Volume 27 (1923)

Shilstone, EN, *Monumental Inscriptions in the Burial Ground of the Jewish Synagogue at Bridgetown, Barbados* (McMillan, London, 1988)

Sharot, Stephen, 'Reform and Liberal Judaism in London, 1840-1940' in *Jewish Journal of Sociology,* Volume 19 (1979)

Spungin, J, *A Short History of the Jews of Nottingham* (Typescript 1951)

Steel, Donald J, (and Samuel, Edgar R) *National Index of Parish Registers, Volume 3: Sources for Roman Catholic and Jewish Genealogy and Family History* (London, Society of Genealogists, 1974)

Stern, Rabbi Malcolm E, *First American Jewish Families: 600 Genealogies, 1654-1977* (Baltimore, Ottenheimer Publishers, 1991)

Susser, Rabbi Bernard, *The Jews of South West England: The Rise and Decline of Their Medieval and Modern Communities* (University of Exeter Press, 1993)

Susser, Rabbi Bernard, *Studies in Anglo-Jewish History: The Decennial Census, Jewish South West of England and Stroud* (London, 1996)

Torode, Father Brian, *The Hebrew Community of Cheltenham, Gloucester and Stroud* (revised edition, Cheltenham, 1999)

Van Wijk, WE, *New and Decimal Tables for the Deduction of Jewish Dates* (The Hague, AM Stols, 1947)

Wenzerul, Rosemary, ed. *Jewish Ancestors? A Beginner's Guide to Jewish Genealogy in Great Britain* (Jewish Genealogical Society of Great Britain, 2000)

Williams, Bill, *The Making of Manchester Jewry* (Manchester University Press, 1976)

Wolf, Lucien, *Jews in the Canary Islands* (London, J.H.S.E, 1926)

Zubatsky, David S and Irwin M Berent, *Jewish Genealogy: A Source Book of Fanuly Histories and Genealogies* (New York, 1997)

INTERNET

The Internet is rich in material relating to Jewish genealogy, history, language and culture.

One of the simplest ways of assessing relevant sites would be to use Cyndi Howells' List (http://www.cyndislist.com) which includes a section simply called 'Jewish'.

Among the more useful sites are the following:

*JewishGen: 'The home of Jewish genealogy'.
http://www.jewishgen.org

*Avotaynu. Major publishers of works on Jewish genealogy.
http://www.avotaynu.com

*International Association of Jewish Genealogical Societies. The Association co-ordinates the work of some 60 local Jewish genealogical societies throughout the world.
http://www.jewishgen.org/ajgs

*The Jewish Genealogical Society of Great Britain.
http://www.ort.org/jgsgb

*The London Jews Database. Compiled by Jeffrey Maynard. Jews who lived in London in the first half of the nineteenth century.
http://www.jewishgen.org/databases/londweb.htm

*Sephardic Genealogy Sources.
http://www.orthohelp.com/geneal/sefardim.htm

*Sephardim.Com.Sephardic genealogy and culture.
http://www.sephardim.com

*Sephardim and Crypto-Judaism: definition of terms and brief history.
By Dr. Seth Ward.
http://www.du.edu/~sward/sephardim.html

*The JewishGen Family Finder. A database of ancestral towns and surnames currently being researched worldwide.
http://www.jewishgen.org/jgff

*The Central Archives of the History of the Jewish People. Jerusalem. Founded in 1938 as the Jewish Historical General Archives. Established formally in 1969.
http://sites.huji.ac.il/archives

*Jewish Records Indexing: Poland. A searchable database of 19th century Jewish vital records from current and former territories of Poland.
http://www.jewishgen.or/JRI-PL

*Jewish Genealogy in Australia.
http://www.zeta.org.au/~feraltek/genealogy

*Australian Jewish Historical Society.
http://www.zeta.org.au/~feraltek/genealogy/ajhs

*Researching Jewish genealogies in South Africa. By Saul Issroff.
http://www.jewishgen.org/infofiles/za-infoa.txt

*Calendar Conversions. Julian, Gregorian, Jewish and French republican calendars. By Scott Lee.
http://www.genealogy.org/~scottlee/calconvert.cgi

There are also a number of relevant mailing lists and newsgroups. See Cyndi's List for details.

REPOSITORIES, ETC.

Some useful addresses and miscellaneous information

Most main libraries and record offices throughout the country have books, and in some instances manuscripts, which can be of use to the Jewish genealogist. The following is therefore only a limited list which may be of use to those seeking information about their Jewish forebears and who may not be aware of these specialised collections.

In order to avoid disappointed visits, it is advisable to telephone or write before visiting any repository to check times of opening. If writing, a stamped addressed envelope should be enclosed.

Beth Hatefutsoth, Museum of the Jewish Diaspora, Tel Aviv University Campus, Post Office Box 39359, Tel Aviv 61392, Israel

Central Archives for the History of the Jewish People, Sprinzak Building, University Campus, Givat Ram, Post Office Box 1149, Jerusalem 91010, Israel

> Undertakes no research but can say what is available about a particular *place*. Letters which contain a family name only cannot be answered as the catalogues are not organised by surname.

Family History Centre of the Genealogical Society of Utah, 64-68 Exhibition Road, London SW7 2PA

> Other centres exist throughout the United Kingdom. Each Centre has a catalogue of all the Society's Jewish holdings which include many copies of Synagogue records, etc. If a needed item is not in the library but at Salt Lake City it can be ordered for a reasonable charge. The person ordering then has first use of the film at the Centre.

Guildhall Library, Aldermanbury, London EC2P 2EJ

> In addition to some Jewish books of interest there are records of some business houses which have been deposited and include some Jewish firms.

The Jewish Agency, Rehov Hamaalot 8, Post Box 92, Jerusalem 91920, Israel.

> This is a search bureau for missing relatives and will locate persons living in Israel.

Jewish Genealogical Society of Great Britain, P.O. Box 13288, London N3 3WD

A rapidly expanding archive of Jews and genealogies

Jewish Museum, 129-131 Albert Street, Camden Town, London, NW1

'Men and Women of Mark in Modern Judae'. This is a newscutting book of over four hundred pages, heavily bound and now indexed. The cuttings were collected and bound by E. de Haas in memory of his wife, Bertha de Haas (born 1831 at Iserlohn, Westphalia and died 4 February 1900). The ways in which these men and women made their mark were not necessarily so outstanding that one should be discouraged from consulting it purely and simply because one's ancestors were not of near royal blood.

Lucien Wolf genealogical collection of family histories.

Gaster Collection

The 'Mocatta Pamphlets'

An extensive library of Jewish reference books (some in Hebrew) including some synagogue histories, lists of members, etc. Many books of genealogical interest and usefulness.

Complete set of *Jewish Chronicle*.

Newspaper Library, (British Library), Colindale Avenue, London NW9 5HE.

Jewish Chronicle, many foreign newspapers in addition to those of the United Kingdom.

Society of Genealogists, 14 Charterhouse Buildings, Goswell Road, London EC1M 7BA. Non-members may use the library on payment of a fee.

Colyer-Fergusson Collection: A large collection of manuscript pedigrees of Jewish families, often with supportive information, newspaper cuttings, copies of wills, monumental inscriptions, etc., the work of Sir Thomas Colyer Colyer-Fergusson, Bt. (1865-1951) and his son Max (1890-1940). There is an index of names.

Hyamson Collection. A large number of typed and manuscript pedigrees, some correspondence, and other lists relating to Jews, the work of Albert Montefiore

43

Hyamson (1875-1954). A detailed index has been compiled by Isobel Mordy.

The pedigrees in the Colyer-Fergusson and Hyamson Collections are also indexed into Zubatsky, D S and I M Berent, *Jewish genealogy: a sourcebook of family histories and genealogies* (1997)

D'Arcy Hart Collection: relates to Jewish families, the work of Ronald James D'Arcy Hart (1895-1985). The names have been indexed by Isobel Mordy.

Mordy Collection: The Jewish genealogical material and some pedigrees compiled and indexed by Miss Isobel Mordy (died 1993) were microfilmed by the Genealogical Society of Utah in 1984. There are copies of the eleven microfilms at the Society of Genealogists. She continued to add to the original collection until it too was passed to the Society shortly before her death.

Document Collection: The Society's Document Collection includes some material contributed regarding Jewish families.

The library also contains many general reference books: directories, poll books, text books, etc. There is a complete set of the *Transactions* of the Jewish Historical Society of England.

The library also holds a set of *Avotaynu: the international review of Jewish genealogy* and various publications on microfiche of the Association of Jewish Genealogical Societies, including the Jewish Genealogical People Finder (containing about 150,000 entries), the Gazetteer of Central and Eastern Europe (with 350,000 entries), the Index to the Russian Consular Records, the Publications of Jewish Genealogical Societies (1977-1990) and other indexes.

The Society for Jewish Family Heritage, 17 Kaplan St. Room 217, Post Office Box 7053, Tel Aviv 61070, Israel.

This exists 'to strengthen the consciousness of belonging to the Jewish People and its spiritual heritage'. It encourages Jews throughout the world to trace their family heritage and has published *Tracing your Jewish roots in London, a personal experience* by Carol Clapsaddle (c. 1987).

The Jewish National & University Library, Post Office Box 503, Jerusalem 91004, Israel.

Yad Vashem, The Holocaust Martyrs' and Heroes' Remembrance Authority, Post Office Box 3477, Jerusalem 91043, Israel.

Will not trace relatives but can say if information on a particular individual (a Page of Testimony) has been submitted by survivors of the Holocaust. A search can be conducted if the family name, first name and place of residence of the Holocaust victim prior to the Second World War is provided.

Naturally you will get the best results by going in person or getting an interested relative to go for you. As elsewhere, if you write to these libraries remember to be quite clear what you want and not to ask for too much. Librarians can only give a little time to each enquiry.

There is also the **International Tracing Service**, Arolsen D-3548, West Germany, which was established in 1943 to help locate displaced persons and to reunite separated families. It will provide the name of the concentration camp in which a person was confined, his or her place of birth, personal information, and the person's fate. The full name and some identifying information must be provided, the name alone is not sufficient.

SOME USEFUL ADDRESSES

*Association of Genealogists and Researchers in Archives (AGRA), 29 Badgers Close, Horsham, West Sussex, RH12 5RU.

Association of Jewish Genealogical Societies (as for Avotaynu), an association of 50 societies, 40 in the United States of America, 4 in Canada, 2 in Israel, and one each in Australia, Brazil, England, France, Holland, Russia and Switzerland. The Societies are listed with addresses in *Avotaynu*, vol 11 (1995), pp 58-9.

*Association of Professional Genealogists in Ireland, c/o Genealogical Office, 2 Kildare Street, Dublin 2, Ireland.

*Association of Sottish Genealogists and Record Agents, P.O.Box 174, Edinburgh EH3 5QZ, Scotland.

Avotaynu: The International Review of Jewish Genealogy, 155 North Washington Avenue, Bergenfield, N.J. 01621, USA.

Bevis Marks Congregation Office, 2 Asworth Road, London W9.

Chief Rabbi's Office, Adler House, 735 High Road, North Finchley, London, N12 0US.

Family Tree Magazine, 61 Great Whyte, Ramsey, Huntingdon, Cambridgeshire, PE17 1HL.

Federation of Family History Societies, PO BOX 2425, Coventry, CV5 6YX.

Guild of One Name Studies, Box G, 14 Charterhouse Buildings, Goswell Road, London EC1M 7BA.

International Jewish Genealogical Resources (IJGR UK), 25 Westbourne Road, Birmingham B15 3TX.

Jewish Chronicle, 25 Furnival Street, London EC4 1JL.

Jewish Echo, 463 Eglinton Street, Glasgow G5 9RT.

Jewish Gazette, 18 Cheetham Parade, Manchester M8 6DJ.

Jewish Gazette, 395 Street Lane, Leeds 17.

Jewish Genealogical Society of Great Britain, P.O. Box 13288, London N3 3WD.

Jewish Historical Society of England, 33 Seymour Place, London W1H 5AP.

Jewish Memorial Council Bookshop, 25-26 Enford Street, London W1.

Jewish Museum, 129-131 Albert Street, Camden Town, London NW1.

Jewish Recorder, 49 Allcock Street, Birmingham B9 4EA.

Parkes Library, University of Southampton, Highfield, Southampton, SO9 5NH.

Society of Genealogists, 14 Charterhouse Buildings, Goswell Road, London EC1M 7BA.

*Bodies of professional genealogists.

Taken from 'Jewish Ancestors? A Beginner's Guide To Jewish Genealogy in Great Britain' (Edited by Rosemary Wenzerul)

GOING FURTHER AFIELD
(EUROPE AND ELSEWHERE)
Saul Issroff

Although this Guide is aimed at research in the British Isles, the following addresses and information may be of help to beginners who are tracing their family abroad. This list is by no means comprehensive.

Major starting points are accessible on the World Wide Web. These include Jewishgen: <www.jewishgen.org> . This is the major resource for Jewish Genealogical information and has a number of detailed FAQ's (frequently asked questions) and links to many other sites of genealogical interest.

The Eastern European Archival Database has the combined archival holdings derived from Belarus, Lithuania, Moldova, Poland and the Ukraine. <www.rtrfoundation.org/archdta.html>

AUSTRALIA

Australian Archives, Queen Victoria Terrace, Canberra, Australia.
PO Box 7425, Canberra Mail Centre, ACT 2610, Australia.

National Library of Australia, Canberra, ACT 2600, Australia.
E-mail: http://www.nla.gov.au

AUSTRIA

http://www.jewishgen.org/BohMor/ausguide.htm. Schoenberg, Randol E, *Beginner's Guide to Austrian-Jewish Genealogy.*

Jewish Birth, Death and Marriage Records, Israelitische Kultusgemeinde Wien

Most of the record books ("Matriken") of Jewish births, marriages and deaths in Vienna from the early 1800s to 1938 have survived and are owned by the Jewish Community of Vienna.

Israelitische Kultusgemeinde Wien, Matrikelamt, Seitenstettengasse 4, A-1010 Vienna, Austria. h.weiss@ikg-wien.at   http://www.ikg-wien.at/

Duplicate versions of the Viennese Jewish Matriken have been microfilmed and are in the Wiener Stadt- und Landesarchiv, Magistrat der Stadt Wien, Magistratsabteilung 8, Wiener Stadt- und Landesarchiv, Rathaus, 1082 Wien. E-mail: POST@m08.magwien.gv.at.

For civil marriage records (from 1870), birth records (from 1868) and death records (from 1872) of persons who did not belong to a religious community (including many mixed marriages and their children), contact: Magistrat der Stadt Wien, MA 61 Zivilmatrik, Rathaus Stiege 8, Paterre, Zimmer 17 C 1, 1010 Wien, Österreich. post@m61.magwien.gv.at

BELARUS

Central State Historical Archive of Belarus, u. Kozlova 26, 220038 Minsk, Belarus. National Center For Archives and Records Management (Belarus) http:// www.president.gov.by/gosarchives/eindex.htm Belarus SIG http://www.jewishgen.org/Belarus/

CANADA

The National Archives of Canada, 395 Wellington Street, Ottowa, KIA ON3, Canada.

CZECH REPUBLIC (Bohemia-Moravia)

http://www.jewishgen.org/BohMor/czechguide.html

Federation of the Jewish Communities of the Czech Republic Maiselova 18, CZ-110 01 Praha 1, Czech Republic. fedzid@vol.cz

The Jewish Museum of Prague has a large collection of Jewish records: Zidovske muzeum Praha, U stare skoly 1, 110 01 Praha 1, Czech Republic. office@jewishmuseum.cz http://www.jewishmuseum.cz/aindex.htm

Czech State Archives: The birth, death and marriage records of the former Jewish communities of Bohemia and Moravia, as well as the Catholic parish duplicates, are located at the Czech State Archives in Prague.
Czech State Archives, Statni istredni archiv, tr. Milady Horakove 133, CZ-166 21 Praha 6, Czech Republic. arch@mvcr.cz

Regional Archives: Czech archives - Central, District, County and City and their branches - are listed on the following website:
http://www2.genealogy.net/gene/reg/SUD/crarch-list.html#g1

DENMARK

Danish National Archives, Rigsdagsgarden 9, DK 1218 Kobenhaven, K. Denmark.

FRANCE

Kallmann, Ernest, *Jewish Genealogy Research In France*
http://www.jewishgen.org/French/kallmann.htm
http://www.jewishgen.org/French/links.htm

National Archives: Archives Nationales de France, 60 rue des Francs-Bourgeois, Paris 3

Cercle de Généalogie Juive (in French and English) http://www.genealoj.org/

GenAmi - International Association of Jewish Genealogy (in French and English) 76, rue de Passy, 75016 Paris - France. asso.genami@free.fr
http://asso.genami.free.fr/

Cercle Généalogique d'Alsace (in French and English)
Archives du Bas-Rhin - 5 rue Fischart, 67000 Strasbourg. cgalsace@chez.com
http://www.chez.com/cgalsace/page_acceuil_anglais.htm

France GenWeb (in French) http://www.francegenweb.org/
Le Judaisme Alsacien (in French) http://www.sdv.fr/judaisme/
Centre de Documentation Juive Contemporaine (in French and English)
http://perso.wanadoo.fr/memorial-cdjc/
SefardSIG: Sephardic Genealogy http://www.jewishgen.org/SefardSIG/

GERMANY

Births, Marriages and Death Registry Offices:
Senatsverwaltung fur Inneres in Berlin
IC 506/507, Fehrbelliner Platz, D-10702 Berlin
No central registry office in Berlin, each district has its own. If the exact address of the district is not known, the above may be of use.

Landesarchiv Berlin, Kalckrreuthstrasse 1-2, D-10777 Berlin
Lists of Berlin deportations, other Berlin Jewish Communal material

State Archive Stuttgart
Konrad-Adenauerstrasse 4, D-780137 Stuttgart. Hauptstaatarchiv@s.lad-bw.de
http:www.lad-bw.de

Generallandesarchiv Karlsuhe
Nordliche Hildapromenade 2, D-76133 Karlsruhe

HOLLAND

Register Amsterdam, Stadhouderskade 85, Amsterdam, Holland, www.amsterdam.nl

Dutch archives online http://www-lias.rad.archief.nl/genlias/ara/logon?cid=-1
Dutch links http://members.tripod.com/~westland/linksto.htm
Dutch Jewish Genealogy http://web.inter.nl.net/users/DJGH/

HUNGARY

Hungarian Jewish Genealgoical Research see http://www.jewishgen.org/Hungary/

ISRAEL

Central Archives for the History of the Jewish People, PO Box 1149, 91010 Jerusalem, Israel.

General inquiries: archives@vms.huji.ac.il, http://sites.huji.ac.il/archives/

Worldwide focus, but strong collections on French, Italian, German and Austrian Jewry. Some records from Eastern Europe.

Jewish National and University Library, PO Box 503, Jerusalem 91004, Israel.
Central Zionist Archives, P.O. Box 92, Jerusalem 91000

General inquiries: cza@shani.net, http://www.wzo.org.il/cza/default.htm

Yad Vashem Martyrs and Heroes Remembrance Authority
PO Box 3477, Jerusalem 91034, Israel, (Archives, library and Hall of Names.
The ultimate resource for Holocaust research)

General Information: general.information@yadvashem.org.il
Information about the Holocaust: holocaust.resources@yadvashem.org.il
Information about victims of the Holocaust: names.research@yadvashem.org.il
Library: library@yadvashem.org.il, http://www.yadvashem.org/

Douglas E Goldman Jewish Genealogy Center
Beth Hatefutsoth –The Nahum Goldmann Museum of the Jewish Diaspora
P.O.B. 39359, Tel Aviv 61392, Israel
General inquiries: bhwebmas@post.tau.ac.il, http://www.bh.org.il/Genealogy/index.asp

The Dinur Center For Research In Jewish History
The Hebrew University Mount Scopus, Jerusalem, Israel 91905
Regional Projects: Romanian Jewry, Hungarian Jewry, Dutch Jewry, Hispania-Judaica,
Germania Judaica. dinur@h2.hum.huji.ac.il
http://www.jewishhistory.huji.ac.il/Internetresources/gen.htm

LATVIA

Central State Historical Archives, Slokas iela 16, LV-1007, Riga, Latvia.
Latvia SIG. http://www.jewishgen.org/Latvia

LITHUANIA

Lithuanian Archives Department, http://www.archyvi.lt

Lietuvos Valstybinis Istorijos Archyvas, (Lithuanian State Historical Archives)
Gerosios Vilties 10, Vilnius 2015, Lithuania.
Pre-1940 vital records and some Revision Lists (census).

Centrinis Valstybinis Civilnis Metrikacijos Archyvas, Kalinausko St. 21, Vilnius,
Lithuania. (Holds vital records from 1940)

Kaunas Regional Archives (Kauno Apygardos Archyvas) Maironio 28A, 3000
Kaunas, Lithuania
This archive contains Pre-1915 records: Revision Lists, Tax Records, Guild Records,
Court Records, and other records

Litvak SIG http://www.jewishgen.org/litvak/

POLAND

Naczelna Dyrekcja Archiwow Panstwowych; ul. Dluga 6, Skr. Pocztowa Nr 1005,
00-950 Warszawa, Poland. (Records over 100 years old are located throughout a

dozen-plus regional archives, but write to main archives listed above). Records less than 100 years old are still stored at the local Civil Registrar's office. Write to: Urzad Stanu Cywilnego, (name of your town), Poland.

Polish State Archives, http://www.archiwa.gov.pl/index.eng.html
Galicia SIG http://www.jewishgen.org/Galicia/
JRI-PL [Jewish Records Indexing Poland] http://www.jewishgen.org/jri-pl

Jewish Historical Institute, ul. Tlomackie 3/5, 00-090 Warsaw, Poland
http:// www.jewishinstitute.org.pl
The Ronald S. Lauder Foundation – Poland: Jewish Genealogy Project, ul. Tlomackie 3/5, Warszawa 00-090 Poland. http://www.jewish.org.pl/english/foundati/Lauder1.html

ROMANIA

Archivelor Statului din Republica Romania, Bdul Kogalniceanu nr. 29, Buceresti, Sect 5, Romania.

SLOVAKIA

Statny Ustredny Archiv, Cesta 42, Bratislava, Slovakia.

SOUTH AFRICA

Central Archives Depot, Private Bag X236, Pretoria, 0001 RSA. National Archives Repository, (Contact: The Head). arg02@acts.pwv.gov.za
http://www.national.archives.gov.za/

Cape Archives Depot, Private Bag X9025, Cape Town, 8000 RSA.
Department of Home Affairs, Private Bag X114, Pretoria, 0001 RSA. (vital records)

Center for Jewish Genealogy and Migration Studies
Kaplan Center, University of Cape Town, Private Bag Rondebosch, Cape Town, South Africa. General inquiries: kapgen@humanities.uct.ac.za
Southern Africa Jewish Genealogy Website http://www.jewishgen.org/SAfrica

UKRAINE

Central State Historical Archives of Ukraine, u. Solomenskaya 24, 252601 Kiev, Ukraine. Tel: (044) 227 3002 Ukraine State Archives: http://www.scarch.kiev.ua
Ukraine SIG http://www.jewishgen.org/Ukraine/

USA

Center for Jewish History, 15 West 16th Street, New York, NY 10011. This incorporates the Center Genealogy Institute, the American Jewish Historical Society Archives, the Leo Baeck Institute, the YIVO Institute and the American Sephardi Federation.

Center Genealogy Institute
General inquiries: info@cjh.org, http://www.cjh.org/family. Web pages include FAQs, a virtual exhibit, a complete list of the reference collection, and pdf files of all fact sheets.

American Jewish Historical Society (American Jewry).
General inquiries: ajhs@ajhs.org, http://www.ajhs.org/libarch.htm

Leo Baeck Institute (German Jewry - history, culture and genealogy)
General research inquiries: lbaeck@lbi.cjh.org.
Family research inquiries: kfranklin@lbi.cjh.org, http://www.lbi.org/

YIVO Institute (Central and East European Jewry)
General inquiries: yivomail@yivo.cjh.org, http://www.yivoinstitute.org/

American Sephardi Federation
General inquiries: mustaev@cjh.org, http://www.asfonline.org/portal/

American Jewish Archives, (American Jewry) 3101 Clifton Avenue, Cincinnati, OH. 45220. USA.

United States Holocaust Memorial Museum
100 Raoul Wallenberg Place, SW
Washington, DC 20024-2126
General inquiries   info@ushmm.org
http://www.ushmm.org/

Church of the Latter Day Saints (Mormons), Family History Library, 30 East North Temple Street, Salt Lake City, UT. 84150, USA. http://www.lds.org

The Hyde Park Family History Library, 64-68 Exhibition Road, South Kensington, London SW7 2PA. Has access to many microfilms of Jewish Genealogical interest.

Naturalisation Records, Immigration and Naturalisation Service, FOIA/PA Section, Room 5114, 425 Eye Street, N.W. Washington, DC, 20530. USA.

Passenger Lists, General Reference Branch, U.S. National Archives, 7th Pennsylvania Avenue, N.W. Washington, DC, 20408. USA.

Passports (before 1925 - National Archives, after 1925 see below) U.S. State Department, Passport Office, Bureau of Consular Affairs, FAIM/RS Room 1239, 22nd and C Streets, Washington, DC, 20520.

U.S. National Archives, 8th and Pennsylvania Avenue, N.W. Washington, DC, 20408.

Irma and Paul Milstein Division of United States History, Local History and Genealogy, The New York Public Library, Humanities and Social Science Library, Room 315S, Fifth Avenue and 42nd Street, New York, NY 10018, USA.
http://ww.nypl.org/research/chss/lhg/genea.html

LISTS OF JEWISH GENEALOGICAL SOCIETIES WORLDWIDE

The International Association of Jewish Genealogy Societies represents over 80 societies worldwide and lists can be obtained from:
Avotaynu Inc., P.O. Box 99, Bergenfield, NJ 07621, USA.
http://www.iajgs.org/members.html

In addition to the JGSs, the following Special Interest Groups (SIGs) are composed of genealogists interested in a specific geographic region.
http://www.jewishgen.org/listserv/sigs.htm

OTHER RESOURCES FOR FAMILY HISTORY RESEARCH

The Miriam Weiner Routes to Roots Foundation, Inc., P.O. Box 1376, Secaucus, NJ 07066-1376. http://www.rtrfoundation.org

Jewishgen Internet Urls
JewishGen, Inc. http://www.jewishgen.org
ShtetLinks http://www.jewishgen.org/shtetlinks
ShtetlSeeker http://www.jewishgen.org/shtetlseeker
JGFF [JewishGen Family Finder] http://www.jewishgen.org/jgff/
Ten Steps to JewishGen http://www.toldot.net/jewishgen.html

Additional Reading

1   Avotaynu, the International Review of Jewish Genealogy
Avotaynu Inc., P.O. Box 99, Bergenfield, N.J. 07621, USA.
E-mail: info@avotaynu.com, http://www.avotaynu.com

2   International SIG Journals - Gesher Galicia, Etsi (Sephardi), Stammbaum
(German SIG), Latvian SIG, Belarus SIG and Southern African SIG. See JGSGB
Library: http://www.jgsgb.org.uk/library1.htm

INDEX